lor,

Molly & Tony.

Christmas, 1949

A

TO

A.F.L.T.

SAY PLEASE

by

VIRGINIA GRAHAM

Illustrated by

OSBERT LANCASTER

LONDON

THE HARVILL PRESS

1949

Printed and Made in Gt Britain
by Hague & Gill at
Pigotts near High Wycombe
for THE HARVILL PRESS *Ltd*
and published by them at
2 3 *Lower Belgrave Street, London* SW1
First published in June 1949
Second impression August 1949

CONTENTS

ILLUSTRATIONS

FOREWORD

THIS IS A BOOK on Etiquette for Ladies, neither of which or whom now exists, as everybody knows; so the whole thing, both from my point of view and from yours, is the most shocking waste of time, and I have really no idea how it happened. The only thing that can be said for it is that it will not help you in the least to be a lady, which is all to the good as I believe it is not a desirable status, but it may make you laugh, which is always nice, even if this, also, is a waste of time. It may, of course, do nothing of the kind, which will be an enormous pity.

V.G.

CHAPTER I

COUNTRY VISITS

ONE OF THE strangest things about people living in the country is that, contrary to all expectations, they are invariably dressed in black *crêpe-de-chine*. This is because they are just about to go to, or have just about returned from, a bazaar or a whist drive. For visiting the local town on a Saturday morning (a regular feature of rural life, you will find—it has something to do with fish), a hostess wears a hat, a pair of clean gloves and carries a bag. Her husband also wears a hat and, for once, the trousers that go with his coat and waistcoat. The etiquette on this occasion is for the city dweller to look as rustic as her hosts look urban, this anomaly being particularly dear to the English heart.

Sartorially speaking, the mention of a country visit affects metropolitan ladies in varying ways, and their preparations for a sojourn in England's greener and more pleasant portions depend largely on the notions they have about the place. Some go to master it, others to be its slave. The masterful type are not prepared to concede any of their town habits and, bracing themselves against the wiles of nature, go to it adorned in city clothes. Owing to the height of their heels the fields can beckon to them with buttercups and the woods woo them with singing birds in vain. Well camouflaged and exquisitely coiffed they may totter as far as a deck chair on the terrace but not one step further, and will gaze from there upon the country with looks of such regal condescension that the very primroses retire behind their leaves. Their opposite numbers show themselves so eager to embrace their mother earth that, the better to please her simple tastes, they whip from off themselves every visible sign of sophistication. In old flannel shirts and corduroy trousers and with shining, wholesome faces they gallop across the wide open spaces on large, brogued feet, and once again the primroses cower back amazed.

To whichever extreme you yourself may naturally incline, it is well, when visiting in the country, to cultivate, or at any rate assume, the virtue of moderation. The normal country house hostess will be equally annoyed with you should you remain static in *crêpe marocaine* or run wild in whipcord. If you persist in pursuing a policy of non-co-operation and utterly refuse to take part in rustic affairs she will be forced to forego them herself, and will feel impelled to spend the moments usually so happily employed looking at cows talking to you about Willie's adolescent troubles. If, on the other hand, you disappear after breakfast and do not return until dinner time covered in mud and with cowslips dangling behind your ears, she will have had to battle by herself with the numerous local bores to whose entertainment and internal nourishment every Sunday afternoon is dedicated. You were to have been the *pièce de resistance*, the something new in a never-changing scene, and she will not look favourably upon your absence.

It is well to remember that although the ostensible purpose of your visit to the country is that you should enjoy yourself, society imposes limits on the amount of enjoyment you can reasonably expect, and it is etiquette here, as in other spheres, for joy to be paid for. An effort, however small, to be companionable and indeed useful to your hostess will earn her lasting gratitude, for although she may have asked you down "to have a good rest", it will not have been her intention that you should lie speechless, in a torpor, for forty-eight hours. Either she will have other guests to whom it is expected you should pass a remark every now and then or else, living as she does during the week solely in the company of cocker spaniels, she may need verbal encouragement herself. Thus if you, in your elegant *imprimé*, reclining on a *chaise assez longue* under a cedar, passing a somnolent eye over the advertisements in *Vogue*, are invited to go and look at the horses, don't say, "I think I'll stay here if you don't mind," because your hostess *will* mind. By the same token, if you come charging into the house after a long day's gambol with the lambs, and your hostess suggests walking across to the Banbury-Wakefields for a drink, don't say, "I think I'll stay here if you don't mind", because again she *will*, very much indeed.

Incidentally, if you have to give a horse a lump of sugar or a slice of carrot, see that it is placed strictly in the centre of the palm of the hand and keep your thumb well back. Owing to the extraordinary length of a horse's nose and the curious position of its eyes, it cannot really see what it is doing and imbibes nourishment by touch system. Sugar, carrots and thumbs are all one to it until they are actually in the mouth when, presumably, they taste differently, so keep the digits as much together as possible so as to form an oblong pink plate. Few horses have eaten a whole hand in one mouthful.

Equally incidentally, few Banbury-Wakefields have

limitless bottles of whisky, so do not remark how thirsty the country air makes you and toss down their potions as though they were made of lemonade. Unless, of course, they are made of lemonade. Even then, for a different reason, they should be drunk in moderation.

On Sunday morning it is no longer *de rigueur* to dress as for Church if one has no intention whatsoever of going there. Not only is it hypocritical but also an infernal waste of time changing again after breakfast. Take garments which either separately or superimposed one upon the other can be worn for walking, weeding, going to a Flower Show, playing Bridge or Dumb Crambo or for doing nothing elegantly but in comfort. You will be notified of any excesses, such as tennis or dancing, in your hostess's invitation, and on its receipt can either find the appropriate garments or refuse the invitation, depending upon the state of your liver.

Remember the houses of others are invariably much colder than your own, even if the thermometer states otherwise, and the richer the hosts the colder the house. This does not mean, however, that ladies should wear cardigans over their evening dresses or balaclavas at breakfast. Neither does it mean that guests are at liberty to shut windows or light fires. The temperature of a house is sacred to its owners and should on no account be mentioned except in the privacy of the bedroom. This applies also to the bath water. If a hostess, knowing she has taken all the hot water, says, "I'm afraid, darling, you had an ice-cold bath?" it is then just permissible to reply in the crypto-affirmative, *i.e.*, "No, honestly, it was awfully nearly hot enough, and I only hope *I* didn't take all the hot water". This is what is known, quite simply, as good manners, and though perfectly useless thermostatically speaking, maintains that atmosphere of goodwill so necessary in human relationships.

The only way to stop teeth chattering is to get warm.

It will be the firm intention of your hosts to take you, as soon as possible, *away* from their homes. Remember, they do not know what on earth to do with you and have been arguing about it for weeks, so do not be difficult and announce that all you want to do is to sit still and look at the view. They are irrevocably determined you should be entertained, and it is a matter of little importance whether you wish to be or whether you don't. In point of fact, life being what it is in the country, it is they who wish for entertainment and the perfect guest provides the perfect excuse. So be prepared for all sorts of pursuits, probably far removed from your interests and certainly far removed from an armchair, and enter into the spirit of them with grace if not with pleasure.

CHAPTER II

BONFIRING

ONE OF THE oldest country house pursuits is that of Forestry. To take part in this traditional sport it is sagacious to borrow some of your hostess's more decrepit garments and to appear in them caught up with a hundred safety pins or, alternatively, with a gaping placket hole.

You will then be taken into a nearby copse and given a billhook. Gentlemen have a very poor opinion of a lady's ability to cut either down or up wood, so you will find the billhook you have been given is blunt. Other implements, such as mattocks with wobbly handles and slightly bent saws, will also come your way, and indeed there may come a moment when you will be invited to dismember a birch tree with a pair of secateurs. On no account should you lay a finger on an axe, neither should you attempt to blaze a trail or open up a vista, for it is a gentleman's prerogative to destroy, and there is nothing more irritating for him than to see a lady cutting down a large tree with the best axe, particularly if she is doing this speedily and accurately. A lady's place in forestry, as well as in all other human experiences, is in the rear, clearing up the mess left by the gentlemen.

As the afternoon progresses and the gentlemen hack their way deeper and deeper into the jungle and advance further and further away from their perspiring *vivandières*, their voices will be heard echoing faintly, albeit a little peevishly, down the rides. "Barbara! Barbara! Do come and hold this damned thing down for me!" "Sylvia, Sylvia! Please come and pull this blasted oak away!" And the ladies, dispersed though they be through the woods gathering damp twigs with which to start a fire, must lift their heads like startled deer and run obediently to do their bidding.

The bonfire, of course, is the nicest part of all, always providing someone can manage to light it. The men, bloodstained and weary, gather round it to smoke their cigarettes, while the women drag forward great branches which they are then urged to cut in half if not in quarters. Fed at the risk of rupture the sparks fly upwards, and also, rather surprisingly, downwards, and there is that strong, sweet smell of singed hair and smouldering Harris tweed without which no bonfire is completely satisfactory. It should be noted that smoke shows a devotion to human beings only equalled by spaniels and will invariably follow them round regardless of the prevailing wind.

At the end of the day, when the thought of tea and crumpets is uppermost in the mind, it is usual to spend half an hour looking for missing weapons; for pipes laid down and not picked up again; for diamond clips that have escaped from bosoms; for left-hand gloves abandoned under bushes and cigarette lighters hidden carefully in arboreal crannies. It is usual, too, for a host to look sadly at the tools used by the ladies and to put them, without a word of rebuke but with the heaviest sigh, into a little straw bag.

Walking back across the misty, twilit fields towards the twinkling lights of the house, the guests, though lacerated and scorched, cannot but rejoice in their accomplishments, for there is nothing, alas, so delightful as destroying things, particularly if they belong to somebody else.

CHAPTER III

HUNTING

A MEET CAN BE one of the loveliest sights in the world, but it is curious how often it takes place in a blizzard. The main thing to strive for, as a pedestrian, is balance. To be too much in the centre of things is to get kicked. To be cowering behind a car is to invite scorn. The very best position to assume is half-way up the bank of a ditch with a small, low car stationed just in front. Leaning the elbows on the roof of this modest rampart it is possible to converse with those on horseback without coming in contact with any part of the horse. If, however, at any time a horse should show an unquenchable desire to suck the sleeve of your coat, it must be permitted to do so, within reason. Reason stops when it uses its teeth.

B

It is usually expected of those guests not on horse-back to keep up with the hunt on foot, or, if there is sufficient petrol, by car. Although this practice has been indulged in for many years it still remains some-thing of a mystery, for though a wide area may be circumscribed, crossed and recrossed, it is only once in a lifetime that contact, either visual or aural, is made with the Hunt after it has once left its Meet. However, this is supposed to act as a spur rather than a deterrent, and at least two hours must be spent in T R Y I N G to find a hound and in T R Y I N G to hear the blast of a hunting horn. It is here necessary to issue a warning. If a fox should at any time approach a hunt-watcher, seeking advice perhaps, or geographical information, this should in no wise be given *out loud*. And in no circum-stances whatever should a fox be invited into a car, as this not only muddies the rugs but also wrecks the fox's day. It is ignorant to suppose that a fox dislikes being chased. A brisk run on a fine morning gives it an appetite, as every hunting man will tell you, and any intention to rescue it from its pursuers, though kindly meant, is misguided.

Hounds are not like other dogs inasmuch as they have sterns like ships and only understand swear words. They are not allowed to talk to onlookers for more than a second because they are supposed to be concentrating on the serious tasks ahead, and a gentle

pat on the nose from a frail though probably frozen female hand has a degenerating and softening influence. Any such contacts are immediately disconnected by a Whip with a whip. This he may flick with only moderate accuracy and it is wiser when he is seen approaching *au grand galop* and *en grande colère* (this also is etiquette) to withdraw a step or two from all dumb friends.

Hounds are never called Rover or Jock like other dogs, but are christened more with an eye to alliteration than to any individual characteristic; thus in one pack you may have everything from Daphne to Dreadnought, and in another anything from Maud to Majestic. As hunting takes place in the open air and is ever so English and ever so traditional, the word bitch can be frequently employed without offence, and indeed it is a rare pleasure for a lady to be able to look fearlessly into the eyes of another lady, even though she be on four legs, and say loudly and clearly "Bitch!"

CHAPTER IV

SHOOTING

ALTHOUGH GENTLEMEN do not like ladies to accompany them out shooting, and although ladies dislike doing so, it was long ago decided that the sexes cannot endure segregation for more than an hour or so, and that at some point in the day's proceedings, usually at the luncheon interval, they should come together again, running towards each other across the fields with little cries like long-lost lovers. This is a darling thought, of course, but the real reason why ladies go out shooting is that they follow the food, few hostesses being either willing or able to provide a meal at home as well as a meal *al fresco*. Shooting lunches are invariably good, but never fail to be draughty as they are partaken of in one of two places: quite simply in the wet, open air or a bit more confusedly in a barn with no door. There are no alternatives. It is wiser for ladies to rely on their garments for warmth rather than to seek an inner calefaction through the medium of cherry brandy, for even if there is sufficient of this ambrosia to go round there is always a danger of becoming over-stimulated and garrulous, this latter being considered a most unbuttworthy condition.

After luncheon the gentlemen, flushed but usually able to stand, take up positions in various exposed parts of the landscape, and it is etiquette that there should then crouch beside them at least one female. No gentleman has ever been known to say "Do come and stand by me", that being the last thing he wants in the world; therefore it is up to the lady to select, with as much speed as is commensurate with good manners, the gentleman who (a) has a shooting stick he will be forced to lend her, (b) is situate short of the ploughed field, (c) is her husband, when anything goes. While waiting three-quarters of an hour for the birds to be stirred up from their arboreal haunts it is permissible to talk, to blow down the gloves, to stamp the feet and to wipe the nose (whimpering is best left to the labradors), but at the first distant noise of beaters beating— surely the most bloodthirsty sound on earth—a rigid paralysis should overtake the watcher. This has often been partially achieved already by the temperature, but it *must* be extended as far as the vocal chords. There is nothing turns a pheasant from its path to destruction as quickly as the sound of a female voice speculating on Fats Waller.

Soldiers' daughters do not put their fingers in their ears, but small, clinging types of civilians' daughters may do so, and shut their pretty blue eyes too if they so desire. But nobody may fall off a shooting stick on to the ground or clasp the shooter round the knees in a paroxysm of nervous grief. These antics can safely be left to foreigners.

Ladies are sometimes hit on the head by moribund birds and almost always hit on the nose by expended cartridge cases. They are also often trodden on by a gentleman seeking to take a high bird, and they are sometimes, though seldom, shot dead by the gentleman next door. There is no pleasure, however, without a spice of danger, and the sound of feathered bodies bouncing on the ground, the smell of gunpowder and the beauty of the wintry trees lashing themselves against the steel grey sky should be sufficient reward for any perils endured.

Birds taste good too.

CHAPTER V

FISHING

VERY LITTLE is known of the etiquette for fishing-watching because only someone deeply in love would dream of doing anything so silly, and lovers are notoriously haphazard about tabulating manners and modes.

In the case of fly-fishing a gentleman often places himself thigh deep in the middle of a river and all that a lady can do is to sit on the bank and look. She must not speak as salmon have very sharp ears, and any remark such as "Darling, you *do* look so sweet" vibrates like a gong through the deeps and puts them off their Jock Scotts at once. As a gentleman will stay anything up to three hours in the water, a lady must have some very beautiful thoughts to sustain her meanwhile, and frankly it is only she who deems each movement of the beloved's wrist a thing of joy, and each little puff from his pipe as part of some divine plan, who can survive the appalling ennui of such a vigil.

Occasionally a gentleman will allow a non-angling lady to "have a go", and it is then etiquette, when the line is dangling weakly two inches out from the bank, for the lady to hook the largest fish that has ever been seen in the Dee since 1892. Unfortunately it is not etiquette for a lady to land this fish. Many attempts have been made to keep hold of the rod, indeed struggles of unsurpassing valour, if of unbecoming appearance, have frequently taken place on the water's edge, the gentleman crying, "No, no, you fool, keep the point up! Oh, for God's sake, give it to me, oh *no*, you ass!" and the lady screaming, "Damn you, I hooked it and I'm going to land it or lose it, I don't care which but it's MINE!" As in all purely physical battles between the sexes, however, the gentleman, if he dare be so called, wins, and if there is anything left of the rod and its addenda, not to mention the fish, which has had a very puzzling experience up to now, he proceeds to land it and claim it as his own. Ladies have to be very much in love to stand this sort of thing, and many a romance has thus swirled away down the rocky path of a Scottish river to be lost in the soulless sea.

There is another sort of fishing, despised by many and yet loved by lovers. The little bit of bread on a hook; the gaily coloured float sitting idly amongst water-lily leaves; the sun on the water; the tuft of midges over the beloved's head; the jam jar on the grass; no hope of anything larger than a roach; the hand in the hand . . . there is much to be said for this, and none of it need be said in a book on etiquette.

CHAPTER VI

RACING

RACE MEETINGS are usually attended by those who like racing, but there are two dates in the Racing Calendar to which ladies who dislike racing intensely should give particular attention. One is Ascot, the other their local Point-to-Point. Neither of these events can be avoided if a lady wishes to be well thought of, for if she fails to attend the former she shows a disrespect for both horseflesh and *couture*, for which lapses society will be slow to forgive, and if she ducks the latter her neighbours will brand her as the sort of woman who *only* goes to Ascot.

For those to whom the front part of a horse is only slightly less frightening than the back there is little to choose between one race meeting and another, save in

the matter of clothes. At Ascot it is etiquette for ladies
to wear a different costume every day and to take
special care to keep their best confections for the day
on which it rains. Although to a great many ladies the
word Ascot acts, sartorially speaking, like six glasses
of vodka on an empty stomach, it is more ladylike to
dress within the bounds of probability. Ascot is not a
fancy dress ball, so it is really wholly unnecessary to go
disguised as Dolly Vardon. Poke bonnets, mittens and
elastic-sided boots can, of course, be hired for a song,
but a lady should attempt to draw attention to her
beauty by less obvious means. Those with lovely faces
should not steer the eye away from them by wearing
hats with the words "I love you" circumscribed in
velvet letters, or hats in the form of pythons with inter-
locking tails entwining the neck, or hats fashioned of
enamelled twigs on which precariously balance humming birds sucking begonias made of *broderie anglaise;*
and those with ugly faces should remember that
nothing they can do will make them any better, so it is
better not to do anything at all except be frightfully
nice to everyone. It is true that the ladies who get their
photographs in the papers are those who have invested
in tartan parasols and taffeta muffs, who are wearing
full evening dress and diamond dog collars, or who
have designed for themselves cossack costumes in
cobalt blue satin, but ladies of sensibility should strive

for smartness rather than notoriety and abjure the favour of the Press in favour of the *chic*. An elegant, well-cut afternoon dress is all that is required; a becoming hat, gay but not hysterically so; plain ungarnished gloves of a pristine appearance and interesting but easily recognisable shoes; on the bosom a handsome brooch from which is suspended the Royal Enclosure ticket and over the arm, of course, the mackintosh.

Far the most important item in this catalogue of effects is the shoe, for there is no other human activity, save perhaps sight-seeing, which is so hard on the feet as racing. To mill about in a large crowd for hours on end is never restful, but when it is necessary to retain an aura of elegance, radiance and youth for *days* on end, it is essential that the feet should be cherished above all else. Those confused and aimless walks to the paddock and round the paddock and back from the paddock and up to the stand and down from the stand and down to the rails and back from the rails and along to the paddock and round the paddock and back from the paddock and so on *ad infinitum*, have to be undergone with the maximum of grace, and there is literally vouchsafed no opportunity whatsoever for removing the shoes. This does not mean, however, that it is etiquette to go in brogues, unless of course they have been especially made in lilac satin stamped with Gordon Richards' face in amethyst sequins on the heels.

As it is not thought seemly that a lady should be polluted by contact with a Turf Accountant, she is not permitted to place bets with bookies while she is in the confines of the Royal Enclosure, but must wait at a becoming distance while her male escort bargains on her behalf with these loud-mouthed carrion of the Course. During this period of abandonment she may get as much rest as she can by standing first on one leg and then on the other, or by leaning on another lady, but on no account must she lie down. If she feels a sudden urge to tear off her gloves and her plastic wimple, to leap the bars of the compound and canter to the other side of the course where so comfortably moil the lower orders in the "short and simple flannels of the poor", she must resist it or forever be cast out from Society. It is largely due to Ascot, for which so few ladies now have the stamina, that Society is in such a parlous condition, for much of the true aristocracy, worn out with washing up, has tossed its heritage aside and gone across the great divide to join the ranks of those who sit on the grass between races, leaving behind it on the right side of the rails the virile *nouveaux riches* to raise their grey top hats in an absurd and insolent fashion.

> *"Oh mourn this traitor to her class*
> *Sporting with the gypsies on the grass,*
> *Here you behold a Countess couchante,*
> *Could anything be quite so touchante?"*

Point-to-points are a very different matter. For one thing they are much colder. The correct dress for such events is lots of tweed, usually of varying lengths and antagonistic shades, Newmarket boots and a felt hat, such as little boys wear at school, into which has been thrust a regimental badge in diamonds. The Lancers have quite a nice badge, and so have the Guards' Regiments. The badges of other regiments, of course, are not so effective.

As there is usually some member of your family, or a friend, or a friend of a friend, riding in a steeplechase there is a certain tension in the air, not unakin to that found in a dentist's waiting-room. Some member of your party is bound to be feeling sick, to be deep in prayer or to be deciding what hymns to have at the funeral. Cherry brandy or sloe gin are excellent antidotes to mental suffering, but it is wise to offer the expectant widow and fatherless a sausage roll at the same time. Intoxicated relatives weaving about the course do nothing to mitigate the natural horrors of the afternoon.

Although it is very difficult to have a picnic lunch in a car, you will find that the weather invariably necessitates this, but if you are all good friends matters can be arranged so that ample space can be made on one of the car seats for the inordinate amount of sandwiches and apples you have brought with you. This accommodation can be provided quite simply by expelling a

c

gentleman from the car and forcing him to eat, standing up, outside in the rain. He can be used as a conveyor belt for dirty plates going from the windows to the roof, and as a dispenser of coffee from the thermos flask he is invaluable. As one-third of the coffee from a thermos is predestined to be spilt, it is the sheerest folly ever to attempt to evacuate it except *al fresco*.

It is not easy to find out where a point-to-point starts, where it ends, or where any of the fences in the middle are situate, but having obtained this information it is etiquette to go and crouch by the side of a jump, along with the St John's Ambulance man, and wait events. Everybody must do this, even the wives of riders. It is disgracefully sissy to stay in the car with the wireless on. If wives cannot bear to look or hear or know what is happening they can just as well shut their eyes, stop their ears and recite the Lord's Prayer in the o p e n. Cowardice should never be encouraged. It is only by overcoming things that Britain holds the truly extraordinary place she does in the world to-day, and in a degree a point-to-point offers an opportunity to overcome nearly all the vicissitudes known to man, fear, cold, discomfort, pneumonia, boredom and indigestion. Let such an occasion be a testing time for English womanhood and let her face it bravely.

CHAPTER VII

FÊTES

IN THE SUMMER one of the first duties of a guest is to profess a great liking for Garden Fêtes, Historical Pageants and Morris Dancing, for there is no Saturday during the summer months when one, or indeed all, of these entertainments is not taking place within easy distance of wherever you happen to be. There is no escape from them, save perhaps in the Hebrides, where the lack of lawn space provides an adequate excuse, and it is an ungrateful guest who does not accompany her hostess on one of these philanthropic peregrinations. As the purpose of such a beano is the raising of funds for some local project as yet ungarnered into the net of nationalisation, it is incumbent upon you to take a reticule in which reposes sufficient cash with which to purchase a jar of pickled onions, a table doyley and some rather wet sweet peas, for whatever the central attraction may be, whether *A Midsummer Night's Dream* acted by the Women's Institute or a Pageant of Youth rendered by the County Guides, it will inevitably be fringed by a mushroom growth of highly collapsible tents under which the natural produce and forced handicrafts of the locality will be offered for sale.

Into this small acreage of space will be condensed the very essence of England. You will find disguised, as befits this levelling age, the ancient feudal system still prevailing, and the gentry, under assumed names, circulating amongst their fiefs to buy a thousand things they do not want for the good of the community. So much a part of England is the Garden Fête that the Englishman abroad, catching by chance in France perhaps, or Italy, a whiff of warm squashed grass, is instantly carried back to the familiar scene; to the heavily mortgaged manor house, the terrace sprigged with thyme; to the smooth lawns peppered with daisies and orange peel; to the striped marquee where claustrophobic roses droop in small green vases, and where in the dim hush the onions, polished with damp cloths, nestle redolently against the scrubbed carrots; to the hoop-la stall bending precariously over the herbaceous border; to the suffocating bathing tent where Mrs

Phipps, in a hired gipsy costume, reads the cards; to the magic shining circle, all red and silver, from which float the tubal strains of *The Gondoliers;* to the wholesome, unconscious faces of his countrymen.

A critical mind is not a good companion to bring to a country Pageant, for ambition oft outruns ability and good intentions art. It is a wise plan, however, to bring an ear trumpet, for the untrained voice rarely has sufficient effervescence to lift itself above the accompaniments of Nature; and many a speech has been drowned by the sound of rooks shouting abuse at one another from the trees, and cows calling to their young in the meadows, not to mention butterflies crashing in and out of flowers and ants banging their way home from work.

Be prepared for the most dramatic moments to founder on rocks which even the ablest producer could not chart, but remember, as a sophisticated smile starts to curl your lip, that even the scenery at Covent Garden frequently collapses, and that before now its mermaids have become inextricably interlocked and its swans frozen in their tracks. Do not expect, when you see Miss Fanshawe come galloping into the arena on Lord Canthorpe's cob, bearing tidings of the imminent approach of Queen Elizabeth —do not expect her to STOP, as the odds are she will ride right past you into the tea tent, and even if Her

Majesty Herself is unable to prevent her charger from paying frequent visits to the White Elephant stall, thereby making it necessary for her to grant the freedom of Stoke Lebanon solely to Mrs Campbell-Porter and her brass *jardinières*, do not mock. It is all too easy to fall into a state of helpless risibility on such occasions, but, as in a church so in a pageant, a *fou rire* is unbecoming. Who knows but that one day you yourself, in the cause of friendship or the Y.W.C.A., may be prevailed upon to don the motley and stand in a wimple in a garden in a gale and proclaim, with as much conviction as possible, that you are Lady Darcy de Snooth waiting for her very parfitt knight to return from the Crusades; and who knows but that he may never return having, through some mechanical defect in his vizor, mistaken the kitchen garden for the arena, and even now canters across it with the raspberry nets he has unknowingly caught in his spurs floating out like brave banners behind him? There on the sward you will remain, holding ye olde bitte of tapestrie in one hand and trying to keep your sugar loaf hat on with the other, and every waiting second will be a torment, every minute a lasting shame. At such a time a careless snigger from a spectator, such as you perhaps have given in the past, makes a wound on the soul that even time disdains to heal; so, with an eye to the future, be courteous and let the girlish ripple of laughter be caught at the very lip by a kerchief which, when stuffed into that ugly orifice you call your mouth, will preserve the decencies very effectively if not very prettily.

Remember, too, that every performer has a family, the members of which, like the arms of a giant octopus, stretch across the width and breadth of the lawn, embracing the 10/6 deck chairs and the 1/6 wooden forms with equal fervour. Men who have garnished their legs with ribbons and bells in order to give a rustic interpretation of the Lancers may strike you as frightfully funny, but these men have mothers. The mothers are not amused. And they are sitting just behind you.

CHAPTER VIII

TENNIS

"She also served but mostly stood and waited."

HARRY GRAHAM

IN ARRANGING a set of tennis it should be remembered that everybody wants to play but says he would much rather not, and that everybody is quite good but says he is the most hopeless rabbit. "No, darling, YOU play. You'd have a much better game without me." "Honestly, I haven't played for years!" and, "Please, I am adamant. I'd MUCH rather watch!" should be repeated in varying keys by all prospective players until someone suggests tossing for it. Ladies should be warned, however, that this is by no means decisive and even when, after spinning racquets for several minutes the desired equality of surface is achieved, protestations of unworthiness should immediately be resumed. It might be assumed in fact that all tennis players dislike the game intensely, or at any rate prefer playing it solo, as in no other sport is there engendered such an apparent distaste for partners and opponents alike. Although it is etiquette to cluster round a damp seat at the edge of the court and argue for ages as to who won't play with who, there comes a moment when this becomes a trifle wearisome and it is then, having adequately preserved the social decencies, that the owner of the court or the person who has hired the court or the least patient human being present should take the matter in hand and issue orders. Dick will play with Joyce and Reggie with Sheila, and let there be no more arguing.

When partnered by a gentleman a lady should spend the greater part of the time speeding back and forth across the back line endeavouring to reach the balls he has missed at the net. Both she and her partner should be permanently sorry about everything as well as running a mutual admiration society expressed in the briefest terms. Long conversations, especially those which have no bearing on the game, should be studiously avoided, as although they have the merit of putting one's opponents off they also put one off oneself. Good shot, bad luck and hell are the five basic words to be used in a game of tennis, though these, of course, can be slightly amplified. Another useful phrase is "Has anyone the *faintest* idea what the score is?" This too can be amplified, sometimes to alarming proportions; indeed it is quite *comme il faut* to fore-gather at the net and discuss with heated politeness and much pointing the astonishing mathematical weakness of the opposing side.

It is never a good plan to blame either one's racquet or one's hostess's balls for the failure one is experienc-cing in connecting the one with the others. Neither are bumps in the court, blinding rain or high winds con-sidered adequate excuses for poor play. Disapproval of the sun's location in the empyrean can be silently ex-pressed by serving underhand and by literally refusing to take lobs. Incidentally, although it is fairly all right to try and win, keenness should invariably be tem-pered with good manners, and balls lofted deliberately into the sun, as well as balls sneaked over the net to one-legged veterans or very fat old ladies, are abso-lutely taboo. This does not apply, of course, to tourna-ment tennis when it is perfectly sporting to volley balls into one's opponents' stomachs or aim them at par-ticularly skiddy patches on the court's surface. Talking of tennis tournaments, it is usual, in the local variety, to call upon neighbourly ladies to act as um-pires, in which case they often find their greatest friends on one side of the net and repulsive outsiders on the other. Doubtless their judgments will be honourable and fair, but in the event of there being a moot point ladies should always concede it to the stranger. Otherwise it looks very much like favouritism. Many ladies' friends have lost tennis tournaments just this way.

CHAPTER IX

INVITATIONS

GONE ARE THE DAYS when it was possible to brood like some pensive hen over an invitation; when slow placid hours could be spent speculating over it, and when the hatching of a plot to refuse it could be incubated in privacy. How pleasant it must have been to write a note on the best writing paper and send it round by a footman, knowing that the lies penned therein lay hidden, eternally secret, sandwiched between that well-groomed heart and that silver-buttoned tail coat. Now, alas, time hovers o'er impatient (besides which there is the small matter of the footman) and there is no kind of escape from Mr Bell's infernal contraption, the invention of which inadvertently caused him to become known as the

Crême des Menteurs. Caught unawares, in bedroom slippers so to speak, and with one's hair down, falsehoods spring as readily to the lips as do frogs into ponds, and the amount of truth talked down a telephone could be balanced on the point of a pin. For it is a fact that although there are only two types of telephonists, those who say yes please and those who say no thanks, both categories, when replacing the receiver, have the definite sensation of having lied. Those who have accepted to go to a dance in Penge are immediately aware that they would rather commit suicide than go, and those who have refused to go to a film *première* instantaneously realise it would be a pleasant thing to do.

It seems as though the quick response demanded by the automatic telephone is answered solely by automatic reflexes, and there being no time for the marshalling of fact *pro* or *contra* an invitation, however graciously extended it may be, the ego falls back on its subconscious and emits affirmative or dissentient cries according to its social or anti-social tendencies. If you cannot follow the thread of this psychological disquisition it is just too bad.

It is, of course, etiquette to appear delighted at being asked to do anything, but it is wise to give an impression of paramount social activity coupled with a, in the circumstances, pardonable addledpatedness;

in fact, you just *must* look in your book. Although this is meant to conjure up a vision of an engagement book, any book will do as long as it rustles a little when flipped. Whatever it is, a bulb catalogue, Roget's *Thesaurus* or, quite simply, A–D of the Directory, hold it near the mouthpiece of the telephone, pause for a second or two and then say "Oh, dash!" in penetrating accents. From then on it is easy.

Most families have, like Oscar Wilde, their Bunburys; mythical fellows who are constantly asking them out to dinner or are arriving from America bearing precious gifts on the very night in question, or are always inconsiderately popping in just as they were putting on their coats to come round for a drink; dear, shadowy men who have never yet failed in the art of friendship and who come and go, get sick and even die at a whim's notice. No house should be without such a man, though it is perhaps more seemly for a lady living alone to have an ephemeral but equally demanding aunt.

It is advisable, after rejecting an invitation on Bunbury grounds, either to stay at home with the cat or to go out with a man who might conceivably be Mr Bunbury, for Fate, having a macabre sense of humour, will almost certainly arrange for you to meet your would-be hosts should you emerge into the outer world. To be seen dancing with Lord Harbinger at the Tic-Tac

a few hours after you were called to Mr Bunbury's
bedside in Lewes is so hard to explain it is hardly
worth trying. Let this be your golden rule—to *live*
your lies to the best of your ability.

Marriage, of course, gives ample opportunity for
procrastination, as each partner can blame the other
for indulging in unbelievably silly pursuits. "I think
we'd love to", you say, "but I have an awful feeling
Tommy is going to an Old Home Guard dinner that
night", or, "Thanks, old boy, but I must just ask
Maria because I have a ghastly idea Wednesday is
Nanny's day off!" The caprices and whims of married
couples can be endless, for failing imaginative prowess
they can cheerfully exchange colds throughout the
year, taking it in turns to lament the other's ill-health
down the telephone. The curious thing, however,
about inventing colds, is that this frequently puts the
idea and the cold into one's head.

After reaching a certain age it is legitimate to throw
etiquette to the winds and be frank. In society, and
indeed out of it, frankness is considered very bad-
mannered, and that is why one has to be of a certain
age before one attempts so drastic a measure. (How
certain the age is can only be ascertained when one
reaches it.) Then, in a voice nicely balanced between
self-depreciation and arrogance, one can say: "No,
Jane! It is sweet of you, but you know how stupid I

am? I simply loathe the country in the winter and nothing in God's earth will make me come to Norfolk in November! I'm sorry, darling. I love you, but NO". This type of remark, firm but loving, resolute but begging sympathy is unfortunately dreadfully wounding, but on reaching that certain age (curse the thing) one prefers, alas, to wound rather than go to Norfolk.

Remember that to get a name for not going out means that eventually you will not be asked out. This is rather a bore, for the whole charm of life lies in being asked everywhere and going nowhere. When you are a very old lady living in one tiny room with only one tiny frayed aspidistra for company, you may wish you *had* gone to Norfolk after all and kept up with dear Jane, who is still being photographed blowing, with her last remaining breaths, down a hunting horn at local Hunt Balls.

Those of you whose inner promptings urge immediate acceptance of every invitation that comes your way would also be well advised to refer to your engagement books, for in the brief time it takes to open them at the right date it may come upon you that, though it sounds the greatest fun to go skating at Wembley with the Protheroes, the fact that you do not know how to skate may considerably detract from the enjoyment. Thoughtfulness in these matters is always desirable, even if the result is the same.

CHAPTER X

DANCES

OWING to this and that, but mostly, it must be admitted, to this, it is rare nowadays for a dance to be given in a private house. Although in many ways this is distressing, to whose who follow Terpsichore on rather faltering feet and who after a couple of hours consider they have jiggled up and down in the same place long enough, it is a blessing, for there is no doubt that it is considerably easier to leave an hotel unnoticed than it is to leave a house. In the olden days the ladies' cloakroom was, save perhaps in Carlton House Terrace, invariably situate at the top of the house and etiquette forbade one to be seen by one's hosts *descending* the front stairs draped in a sapphire blue cloak at eleven-thirty, unless of course one was supported by a friend holding a bottle of smelling salts. Many ladies, determined from the start not to enjoy themselves, endeavoured to leave their coats in the downstairs "Gentlemen's" so that they could be plucked up and carried away into the outer air without anyone seeing, but their efforts were frequently frustrated by the august personages hired for the evening to mix up the gentlemen's hats. "The Ladies' Cloakroom is *upstairs*", they would say, and up one had to go. If, after a passage of time, the sight of her fellow guests sitting in layers down the front stairs banked by silver bowls filled with cigarette ends became too much for a lady, the only means of retreat open to her were (*a*) to hide in the lift until a friendly accomplice told her her hostess had taken the Peruvian *Chargé d'Affaires* into supper, or (*b*) to go home without her wrap. This latter method of dealing with the problem called for a certain courage, for all nights, without any exception, have following mornings, and it was then not always easy for a lady to explain over the telephone how it came about that she so forgetfully left the sapphire blue on her hostess's bed.

In pre-war days dances were so numerous and the faces which haunted them so familiar it might almost be said that life was one long ballet. Save for a brief interlude for luncheon, eaten with ten other ladies at least, a lady spent most of the day in bed, and except at week-ends the rays of the sun were not permitted to approach her sheltered person. Rarely did she see a gentleman in day clothes or talk to anyone, save her *couturier* and hairdresser, without the accompaniment of a dance band, for she had not the strength to rise before 11.30 a.m. and fell back exhausted on to her bed again *circa* 3.30 p.m., the intervening hours being spent telephoning Guards' officers to invite them to dinner three months ahead. Nowadays, however, the flower of English womanhood is largely vertical and can be seen groping its way to work at nine o'clock to peer through half-sealed eyes at the keys of its typewriter.

The young of to-day do not know how blessed they are, neither do they know how much they are to be pitied. On the credit side they have the advantage of not being *blasé* and thus, in contradistinction to their mothers in the turbulent thirties, expect to *enjoy* a dance. Although they have never known the exquisite pleasure of bacon and eggs served on the dot (and never a moment before) of 2 a.m., they have been spared those little beige mice tasting of jellied cardboard through whose meagre breasts was impaled the lie "Quail". They do not have anguished hours wondering whether they dare wear the pink georgette again, for they have no choice but to wear the blue, the white and mother's old *moiré* cut down by Miss Tibbett; and yet their young eyes are surely the poorer for having missed a ballroom trimmed with swirling, floating yards of the finest material shaped by the finest hands?

Life in former days was made hideous by the struggle to obtain—and having obtained to retain—the presence of some twenty or so young people for dinner before a dance. As it was necessary to book many months in advance, many fell by the wayside before the appointed date, particularly gentlemen, who unfailingly discovered they were on piquet or, alternatively, had boils on their necks, twenty-four hours before. It was then necessary to summon uncles to one's aid, and every girl with a grain of intelligence saw to it that her parents were members of large families. Failing uncles, it was the duty of a father to retire into his sitting-room with an egg on a tray, but, as he enjoyed doing this enormously, it was not to be encouraged. Now that space is confined and there are next to no eggs, things are much simpler, and it should not be beyond the power of an average hostess to gather six chicks into her nest, there to nourish them on soup, snoek and tinned grapefruit prior to the "Buffet Dance. (Please bring your own bottle)" which her sister-in-law is giving in the Oyster Room at Gudgeons's Hotel.

To whatever generation a lady belongs the eti-

quette to be employed in going out to a dinner party remains the same. She should try not to fall down her own stairs or up the stairs at the other end. In the vehicle which is transporting her from her home to the appointed place she should sit with her arms above her head so that the blood in her great red hands runs to her elbows, where it may, or may not, gather in large red blobs. As she cannot see these she need not concern herself with their appearance. On shaking hands with her dinner hostess a young lady, however shy, should have ready an observation other than "How do you do?". "Gosh, am I late?" or "You did say eight, didn't you?" will meet the case admirably, being neither provocative nor startling. It is usual for the male members of a party to stand in a little clot at one end of the room and to show a marked disinclination to speak to any of the ladies, but as most rooms nowadays are of cat-swinging dimensions this desire for segregation is constantly baulked, and indeed, on occasions being so to speak, nearly mouth to mouth with a member of the fairer sex, a gentleman may find himself compelled to give utterance to even his most secret thoughts concerning the weather. "Jolly hot, isn't it?" he may say, and a lady must be quick to counter this shrewd observation by saying something equally apt, such as, "Yes, isn't it?"

The young should be taught that the art of conversation is based, quite simply, on talking, and that at a party it is much better for them to say an inordinate number of foolish things than to remain silent until they can think of something worth saying. The number of sensible remarks passed at a dinner party can be balanced on the prong of a fork, but above all things a dinner should have an air of vivacity, and as long as lips are forming words it matters little what inanities they are expounding. In default of anything more orthodox a lady should recite one of Lord Tennyson's poems rather than be dumb. Along with Domestic Science, Citizenship, Stenography and How to Arrange Flowers, a young lady should learn, and having learned remember for the rest of her life, that no question, however simple, should be answered by the word Yes or the word No, but rather by the words Yes and . . . or No but . . .

No one can deny that from a lady's point of view the prevalent fashion of encircling a ballroom with small tables so that it is impossible to distinguish it from a nightclub is a blessing. Abandoned by a gentleman who wishes to dance with a blonde, she need no longer stand by the door searching with anguished eyes for some imaginary partner, nor need she retire to the cloakroom, there to powder her nose as it has never been powdered before, so slowly, tenderly and carefully. She can just stay where the gentleman left her, behind a nice round table covered with a nice clean cloth. Sitting there, alone or with other feminine flotsam, she will find herself able to eye the dancers as from another planet. It is evident she has no wish to join them and evident to all but the most obtuse that there is a man somewhere around getting her a drink from the buffet. The buffet is crowded. That is why he is so long away. The table, like a great, white shield, protects her from the insolent glances of women who have found partners, and she can gaze, for long, thoughtful minutes, into the bottoms of at least fourteen half-filled glasses of champagne or, to be absolutely accurate, cider cup.

There are still some dances, however, where the ballroom retains its former naked appearance and where, save for a few gold chairs amply covered by duennas, there is no equipment for the comfort of unpartnered young ladies. After huddling by the door like a herd of Southdowns in the vain hope that the wolves knocking back whiskies in the bar may care to attack them before the music ends, it is etiquette for these ladies to wander miserably from room to room in couples. On no account must they be found reclining in armchairs in a sitting-room, talking happily to each other or reading *Pride and Prejudice* out loud. If they are not pretty enough to find partners they are certainly not pretty enough to have chairs, of

which there is always a lamentable shortage, and, like
souls lost in Purgatory, they must remain on their feet,
ever straying who knows whither and seeking who
knows what. Ladies of riper years, of course, are less
sensitive to the dictates of etiquette, but, though they
may park their fannies wheresoever they fancy, they
should never, however grievously bored they may be,
either read or knit during a dance. It is, quite frankly,
not done.

Mothers of daughters who have just come out
should take particular care to disregard their young,
and should these disappear for several hours must remain in a state of refined coma on chairs near the band.
Gone are the days when mothers could have six sup-
pers in succession, and they must be thankful when an
elderly beau brings them a bridge roll stuffed with
meat paste, leaning, on the same plate, against an
emerald green jelly. Manual and facial signs to their
offspring should be studiously avoided, for mothers
are always irksome things and when, by pointing
meaningly at their own shoulder-straps or ostentatiously fluffing out their greying hair, they seek to
draw their children's attention to straying under-
clothes and plastered fringes, they are too tedious for
any words. However, though maternal contact is un-
desirable, should a daughter's knickers fall off in the
ballroom a mother is permitted to fold them up and

put them in her bag.

At all the best functions it is now etiquette for at least six out of every eight dances to be Highland Reels. This ensures that the minimum amount of people employing the maximum amount of space should have a thoroughly delightful time. During the execution of these flings it is *de rigueur* for the hundreds of guests who are not participating to stand four deep round the edge of the room. Though frequently stung to tears by the flipping coat-tails of cavorting gentlemen, if not actually knocked down by Junoesque ladies who have been flung too far, they must remain where they are and look as though they liked it.

There is no sadder time in a lady's life than when she is staying in a house in which a dance is being given. During the long day before the night, while the furniture is being re-arranged and room after room becomes uninhabitable, it is borne in upon her that even in the unlikely event of her enjoying the damned thing, the very last guests—yes, even the one who is doing tricks with a champagne bottle and the other who has just drunk its contents—must have left the house before she can go to bed. Time and again during the evening she will find herself sitting out with a gentleman on two gilt chairs planted exactly outside her bedroom door, but though she may gaze wistfully at its panels, and even perhaps fondle its knob, she must never, never cross the threshold. Down she has to go again into the confusion, into the *macédoine* of strange faces and convivial noises, while up here, separated by a plank of eau-de-nil wood, there is a little pool of quiet in which doze the old familiars; the toothbrush, never before so dear; the hot water bottle in its shabby cover; the nightgown; the softly ticking travelling clock. Only by pleading an indisposition of a violent character, such as double hernia, double pneumonia or a double back, can a lady hope to gain the privacy of her bedroom at a reasonable hour, and even those who have been fortunate enough to develop these complaints have, before now, discovered their rooms to be more public than they supposed. A hostess likes her house guests to be in at the finish, but if any lady imagines she can take a nap on her bed for a couple of hours in the middle of a dance and appear looking reasonably composed in time for John Peel she is mistaken.

Only ladies with stamina should go to Hunt Balls, as they are apt, like Charles 11, to take an unconscionably long time a-dying, and are usually held under somewhat severe conditions. It is customary for ladies to be driven anything up to fifty miles to attend one of these functions, over slippery roads under an ice-bound moon or, alternatively, over fog-bound roads under no moon at all. Cold and half asleep, a lady does not look her best when she arrives. Added to which, most Hunt Balls are given in buildings designed for other purposes, such as the local Corn Exchange, the Magistrates' Court, or the British Legion Hall, and although the promoters may have done their very best to make the place look homey by hanging foxes' masks on the walls and trailing paper streamers from cornice to cornice, they do not always succeed in their endeavour. Added to which these buildings are frequently draughty, so that it is inadvisable for a lady to leave her fur tippet in the marquee especially erected in the forecourt for this purpose. Added to which the hygienic, gastronomic and sitting-out arrangements may tend to be inadequate, so really a lady has to be in a very jolly frame of mind before she embarks on such an enterprise. Let it be understood that there is never a question of "popping in" to a Hunt Ball. It is etiquette to arrive when the band is tuning up and to leave after "God Save the King". Hostesses who have paid good sound money for nice pink tickets never leave before they have had a tremendous gallop round the room, their pearls leaping up from their bosoms to strike them on the nose, and blood-curdling cries issuing from their mouths.

At Hunt Balls it is etiquette for all those under sixty to throw bread pellets at one another during supper, and if there are any stairs handy to slide down them on tea trays. It must be remembered that hunting is a blood sport, and that its commemoration is naturally a little bit bloody. Ladies who are not prepared to be boisterous in uncomfortable surroundings would be well advised to keep their soft ways and miserable faces at home.

E

CHAPTER XI

THE THEATRE

WHATEVER etiquette has to say about the matter, it remains now as it was in the beginning and ever shall be, extremely bad manners to be late for a play. It is all very well to come trailing down the aisle in a taffeta crinoline followed by a gentleman smoking a large cigar; it is all very fine and very elegant, but however dazzling you may be, however lovable, kissable or desirable, nothing can alter the fact that, if you are late, you are a sanguinary bore. Like a tired wave Row D rises and falls as you force your way through, and though you may say, "I AM so sorry" to every person you pass, the clang of the seats going up, the whump of the seats going down, the thud of handbags falling on to the floor and the muffled cries of those

whose faces have been grazed by your behind proclaim you are a bore.

Sometimes, of course, circumstances over which
only the ticket agencies have control prevent you from
gaining your seat before the rise of the curtain, for it is
etiquette in some theatres to issue a duplicate set of
tickets to a fairly large proportion of the audience so
that the largest amount of money should be coined for
the smallest number of seats. The clarification of this
problem usually takes one act and, as it can only be
achieved by oral communication, it is kinder to the
rest of the audience if the argument takes place elsewhere than on the actual spot. Should you and the pro-
gramme-seller be conversant with the deaf and dumb
language it is, of course, another matter.

It is well not to be too disheartened should you find
two odious-looking people sitting in your seats, for it
is apparently etiquette in some circles, including your
own, to (a) go to a play on the wrong night, (b) sit in
the stalls with dress circle tickets (incidentally it is
interesting to note how few people sit in the dress
circle with tickets for the stalls), (c) go to the wrong
theatre. These things get sorted out eventually and the
seats of the righteous are rendered unto them.

It is usual for very small people to sit behind very
tall people, but that does not mean that very small
people should take very big air cushions with them. In

fact it does not mean a thing. It is just bad luck.

On the love of all you hold most dear; on your honour as a Brown Owl; on your integrity as a Committee member for Queen Charlotte's Ball, or simply on your life as a Drone, s w e a r, here and now, you will not t a l k during a performance. Smoke, sleep, fidget or eat peppermints if you must, but d o n o t t a l k. There is not one single person in the theatre who has paid money to hear you do so and not one living soul therein who is interested in your trip to Switzerland. Nor is anyone interested in Dame Edith Evans' likeness to your Aunt Mary, nor in Sir Ralph Richardson's amazing resemblance to that man——oh *you* remember——that man who told such wild tales about Tibet——no, darling, he wasn't called Wade——more like Bradshaw? Doubtless both Dame Edith and Sir Ralph have prototypes in this world and it is lovely to think that you know them, but for those who have come to see and hear them act, the good news, if given out during one of their most moving scenes, will be received coldly. Information on anything, unless perhaps it be incipient appendicitis, should be kept for the *entr' actes*.

In the old days it was considered very second-rate to partake of nourishment during a performance, unless one was under fifteen, when one was permitted to have a glass of lemonade or an ice, but now, when the demands of the inner man are both peremptory and recurring, anything goes from sausage rolls in paper bags to full-blown picnic baskets. Inveterate theatre goers have to some extent disciplined their internal rumblings which, at the beginning of the last war when theatres put back their times of opening, echoed so embarrassingly down the aisles, and they have trained themselves to repulse the pangs of hunger which bite so painfully at the entrails *circa* eight o'clock; but those who do not often visit a theatre may suffer hideously unless they are gastronomically fortified at some point during the evening.

Actors have for long been accustomed to the crash of falling tea trays at matinées and they are now rapidly becoming inured to other festive sounds during the evening performances. The tinkle of coffee cups, the rasping sound of biscuits being scrunched, the chink of money passing up and down the rows, the crackle of cellophane paper and the loud whispers attendant upon all these prandial preparations form a background to their every word. There is, however, a limit to their patience, and should these noises continue for more than ten minutes at the beginning of each act they may show marked signs of neurasthenia, some of them, but not—let us be frank—many, going so far as to walk out of their lovers' arms to the footlights, there to administer verbal rebuke to the jugglers of crockery in the auditorium. Even if they do not go to this extreme the noise of a hundred jaws chewing lettuce will fray their nerves to such an extent they may well forget their lines, or, remembering them, may interpret them falsely, shouting when they should be tender and speaking soft words of love in angry, high-pitched voices.

It is good manners, if nothing else, to pretend you have not already seen the play at which you find yourself, but having once embarked upon the ship of ignorance you must take great care not to disembark in mid-stream. Even if you do not give yourself away verbally there are other hazards. To place the fingers in the ears long before there is a sign of a revolver on the stage is highly suspicious, as also is a merry burst of laughter *before* a joke has been made. If you do not feel able to sustain a role of innocence for two and a half hours, stop before you begin, for here, as with expectant mothers, it is a case of all or nothing. If needs be, tell your host you saw the play ages and ages ago when it first came on and that you adored it and have been longing to see it again ever since. If it has only been on a week it is rather difficult to press this point home with any assurance, but really there is no alternative. It is quite out of the question to say, "I saw this play the day before yesterday, and it is absolutely rotten!" Let love be without dissimulation by all means, but not Society.

At some moment in her history a lady will be taken behind the scenes to visit a star, and this, in spite of her sophistication, may prove so exciting she will find herself for once totally unnerved. To be faced, and closely faced, as dressing-rooms are never larger than small bathrooms, with a creature whom she has just seen ranging the human emotions in a very extravagant manner is akin to being faced with Royalty. It is hard to believe he is a human being. Owing to the agitation in which she finds herself, and which the brief trot from the front of the house to the stage door has done nothing to lessen, coupled with the heady smell of greasepaint which rolls along the stone corridors, not to mention the distant view of the backside of an indefinable piece of scenery; with all these ravishments she may well lose her head and become as flustered as a fourteen year old. (If, of course, she is fourteen years' old, she merely becomes imbecile.)

The first thing to remember is that people on the stage look much taller than they really are. If it so be that the six foot god you have worshipped for many a year turns out to be but five foot six, be disappointed if you like, but on no account remark upon it. "Oh, I thought you were much taller!" is an offensive observation, even if the additional inches you had in mind would have precluded the actor from taking the boards at all. Actors are hyper-sensitive and the weeniest denigration hurts them quite dreadfully. They are the least confident of mortals and without praise they wither up and die. It is etiquette, therefore, to lavish upon them as many compliments as time permits, and while we are on the subject of time, do not stay more than ten minutes in any one dressing-room, as every actor worthy of the name has a date at The Caprice at 10.30. As a lot of facial repair work has to be done before then, the layers of sunburn scraped away, the *toupet* removed and the sideburns ripped off a long-winded visitor is unwelcome. If, however, long-windedness is deplored, over-effusiveness is cherished, and a gulping, gasping string of laudatory comments, always, of course, strictly personal, as no actor likes to be reminded of other actors, is greeted favourably. Let there be no buts. "I am still trembling with excitement from that last scene, but I do wish they hadn't made you speak your lines into a handkerchief", or "I adore that divine Hussar uniform of yours, but surely you ought to wear the sword on the other side?" are statements that can well be left unsaid, even if they are spoken with a patent desire to improve the production.

As well as looking taller than they really are, actors on the stage sometimes appear to be younger, but however old they may strike you when you see them close to there is never an occasion on which you can ask them whether they saw Sarah Bernhardt at the height of her triumph. Sometimes an actor who has been on the stage for forty-five years will volunteer the information that he once saw her when he was a boy and she was an old, old lady with a wooden leg, but on no account should this epic moment be taken for granted. Avoid, too offering gratuitous insults to the profession by relating how earnestly you have longed to go on the stage but that your parents didn't think it was a very nice thing to do and that anyway you probably wouldn't have been a success as ladies hardly ever are, are they?

In asking for an autograph it is etiquette to say it is for a small nephew ill in bed, for though all actors simply love writing their names, in asking them to do so you should imply that it is a pretty silly business only, of course, nephews who are both small and ill must be pandered to, ha, ha, thanks very much, he will be *so* delighted. Concerning the value of autographs, and in this particular instance an autographed photograph, there was once a famous actor who received a request from his son at school asking him to send two photographs of himself immediately as he wanted to swop them with another boy for a photograph of a frog climbing out of a hole. The savage thing about this request was that the frog rated not one, but two, photographs.

It is not considered "*bien*" to leave coats and umbrellas in a theatre cloakroom. The longer you live, in fact, the more will you realise that ladies and gentlemen lead extraordinarily uncomfortable lives. A gentleman's hat and coat should be laid under his seat so as to form a footrest for the lady in the stall behind, and a lady should drape her coat over the back of hers so as to form an ash-tray. As a matter of fact it will not stay there for very long but will creep stealthily down her back until she is leaning against hard, pleated ridges, with the sleeves and skirts winding themselves in hot congesting folds about her person. Her hat, bag, fur and library books must be nursed on her lap.

On taking friends to the play it is customary to buy each of them a programme. *En famille* one is adequate for six persons.

Although a cinema invites confidences and the darkness may tend to make you think that you and your friends are invisible and inaudible, it is wiser to remember that this is not in the least true. Ladies may, of course, hold hands with gentlemen, but their heads should remain erect and facing frontwards. The strains of the mighty Wurlitzer, followed by canned crooning, may have an aphrodisiac effect on the system, but there is, *parbleu*, a time and a place for everything and you are fooling yourself if you get the impression that the Empire is the perfect *nid d'amour*.

The night is young. Restrain yourself. Hold everything.

When accompanying elderly relatives to the cinema, you must be prepared for them to lose track of the plot quite early on and to fail to differentiate between the various blondes who claim their attention. Although talking in the cinema must be deplored as a pastime, a certain laxity can be permitted in the interests of consanguineous duty, for it is always better to incur the displeasure of strangers than to risk being cut out of a dear one's will for having shouted "Oh, shut *up*, Aunt Maud!" Thus, when Aunt Maud says "And who is *this* pretty girl, dear?", you can tell her it is the same one who stole the bonds only now she is wearing a hat. Symbolism is as confusing to the aged as it is to children, but when Aunt Maud demands an explanation as to why there is a cavalry brigade charging across the piano keys, it is better to postpone it until the film is over. The flashback is equally bewildering to the unresilient mind, and it is helpful to whisper or, of course, if absolutely necessary, shout: "This is what the young man in the grey suit remembered happening to him ten years ago when he first met the girl who sang that song in the night club". If the old lady mumbles "*What* did you say, m'dear?" just give her gnarled and mittened hand an affectionate squeeze and pass her an acid drop.

CHAPTER XII

THE BALLET

CONCERNING the ballet, the only really important thing to remember is that Pavlova was a Swan and that she was it for about thirty years. It is thus perfectly in order to assume that any middle-aged friends you possess saw her exquisite flutterings. This assumption does not set a cygnet upon their age as does the mention of Sarah Bernhardt or, of course, Mrs Siddons, or, even more of course and considerably more to the *pointe*, La Carmargo; but all the same they will probably be pleased if you pretend they are too young to remember any ballerina before Moira Shearer.

Two further names should be at tongue's tip. Karsavina and Nijinsky. Nijinsky danced in something

called *Le Spectre de la Rose*, and he is especially mem-
orable for having, in the course of this ballet, elevated
himself with a bound into the air and, defying the law
of gravity, to have remained there for a considerable
time. Ballet enthusiasts are divided into two classes;
one which saw him do this with their very own eyes,
and one which didn't see him do it and frankly doesn't
believe he *could* have. You can take your choice.

Another dancer you might just have heard of is
Isadora Duncan who, earlier in the century, wandered
about the stage on bare feet waving large motoring
veils. She was *not* a strip-tease artiste but a very serious
person with a terpsichorean message, and she founded
something, either a school or a method or perhaps
both, which influenced other things that followed
after. So she is important.

The term Central European School means that the
performers dance on their flat feet and either can't or
won't get up on their toes.

It is always odious to draw comparisons, but you
can take it for granted here and now that no compari-
son at any time should be drawn between Fred Astaire
and Massine. Neither is it etiquette to comment on the
undeniable fact that the chorus at the Coliseum dance
much more *together* than the Corps de Ballet at Sadler's
Wells.

It is well to know the names of a few steps even if

you are unable to recognise them, as it is always lady-like to appear knowledgable. The fifth position or *cinquiéme situation* with which you at your dancing class began each revolution, and without which you would have got on so very much better, is not employed much in ballet circles. The *pirouette*—that giddy old friend—is there, and so is the *chassée*, but if these are the only two words you know they are not enough. There is, for instance, the *pas de chat*, the *pas seul* and the *pas-de-deux*. There is not, however, a *pas du tout*. Then there is an *entrechat*, not to be confused with an *entresol*, which is a sort of fish; a *glissée;* a *cabriole* and an *arabesque*, and then you can have, if you feel in the mood for it, a *jeté* or even, daring thought, a *jeté croisé*. Heaven and Madame Rambert knows what any of them signifies, but as long as you memorise them and *jeté* them out at intervals or, to be more precise, in the intervals, you will show you have drunk deep at the Fonteyn of Balletomania.

By the way, it is etiquette for balletomanes to be absolutely positive that there is only one person in the world who can dance a particular part, and should they be forced to witness the circumambulations of his or her substitute they must bury their faces in their hands and refuse to look. Partisanship is the very life-blood of the ballet. And so, of course, in a more vulgar and commercial way is the unbelievable devotion accorded by its neophytes who return night after night to the same theatre to watch the same people dance the same ballets in the hope, one must suppose, that eventually *somebody* will fall down.

CHAPTER XIII

INDOOR GAMES

IT IS ETIQUETTE for those who abhor indoor games to profess a liking for them. This is really the only course open to them as any complaint they make goes unheeded and therefore all they succeed in doing is being slightly unpleasant. It is a curious thing that though three-quarters of the people in a party have no histrionic or literary ability and are both incapable and unwilling, the desires of the fourth quarter prevail; and it is equally curious to note that once a game has started it is always enjoyed by everybody. It is the initial news that is so nauseous and induces cramps in the stomach, hysteria and other nervous disorders.

In choosing sides it is correct to select the people

F

one likes the least or who will obviously be duffers or, of course, one's host. This proves beyond cavil that one is not playing the game to win, which is a very un-English thing to do, but is prepared to take a sporting chance.

The disadvantage of block competitive games is that so much of one's time is spent in the front hall. Although on entering this zone it is in order for a lady to don a fur cape, it is ill-mannered for her to be found, when summoned by her host to "Come in now", wearing his overcoat and a travelling rug, unless of course the game is Charades, when it can be laughed off somehow. It is exceedingly difficult to think of an historical character in a cold front hall, and many a clump has been found after a considerable passage of time, sitting on the stairs in an advanced stage of *rigor mortis*; but the hours expended in this way can be greatly reduced if only one or two members of the group put forward ideas. "Don't you think it would be more amusing if I went in backwards?" or, "Couldn't we make Mark put his trousers inside his socks?" and similar suggestions are, if amplified by a number of voices, guaranteed to promote such an atmosphere of irresolution that it may be well past midnight before any decisive move is made. As the main object of the game is to return as quickly as possible to the bosom of the drawing-room, in whose warm softness the other

guests lie lapped, sucking toffees and trying not to go
to sleep, cleverness is of little value, and it is best, if one
must think of an historical character, to think of Queen
Elizabeth or King Alfred, quite simply and boldly,
and not bother too much about Pepin le Bref or Lud-
wig of Bavaria or Lady Jane Grey, the impersonation
of whom demands time and thought and is rarely
recognisable even if the guessing guests are sufficiently educated to have heard of them.

Occasionally it is necessary for a hostess to spring
tactfully into a breach which might otherwise gape
embarrassingly, *i.e.*, when it becomes evident that one
of her guests has never heard of the Duke of Welling-
ton, when a lady breaks her shoulder strap imitating
Lindwall, or again, when a gentleman drops off and
snores; but any lady with a spark of social sense will be
swift to smooth over any awkwardnesses and will
come gaily forward with the necessary laugh, safety-
pin or nudge in the ribs.

It is usual to play romping games like Kick the
Bucket and General Post in one's best clothes, and it is
etiquette to enjoy the minor accidents concommitant
with these sports, ranging as they may do from gin on
the georgette to broken legs, as all part of the fun.
Hostesses, too, must learn to laugh heartily when the
china cupboards fall flat on their faces and ink-pots
reverse themselves on to the Aubusson.

WRITING GAMES. Writing games should be heralded
by loud cries of dismay coupled with assertions of illi-
teracy and ignorance of all painters beginning with P.
Any hostess who suggests paper games starts at an un-
fair advantage, for she has probably played them so
often she has an encyclopaedic knowledge of every
author, racehorse, statesman and precious stone, not
to mention every rhyme in the world. She also probably knows the difference between a noun and a verb,
and has learnt after years of practise, how to draw a
hippopotamus's legs. Guests can but suffer and endure, and indeed it is a poignant sight to see Ambas-
sadors, Cabinet Ministers, divas and debutantes clen-
ching their pretty teeth over the tail ends of pencils as
they struggle to concoct a novelette out of seventeen
nouns ranging from tapioca to spume without using
any conjugated parts of speech.

The only comforting thing about writing games is
that the brilliantly clever do not by any means excel at
them, and because a man may have written a book
called *Democracy, How Now?* it does not mean he can
knock off a limerick or name a film star. Courage
should be the keynote. It is often necessary to invent
things, but when challenged they should be held to
with resolution. If questioned as to the actual existence
of a poet called Bernard Ruffle the etiquette is to look
surprised and even shocked that your questioner has

not heard of him, and there is no reason, except that it is untruthful, why you shouldn't recite the first line of his poem called *Sea-bed:*

> *Deep, deep sun-glutted arsenical green*
> *pool of the which-ways ravished fish bedecked, etc.*

No one will dare deny his existence after this, only, of course, it is rather a tiring way of winning a point. It is also cheating. The erudite are more likely to get away with this sort of thing, but even the simple can invent minerals called crash and prolixite or rivers called Emmel and Sière without risk of apprehension, always providing they are willing to give graphic and determined descriptions of their components or whereabouts.

It is not etiquette for there to be a sufficiency of pencils to go round or that those provided should have points. This proclaims spontaneity on the hostess's part, even if she decided weeks ago that writing games should be played on the night in question.

A time limit should be arranged for the conclusion of each game, to which on no account should the players adhere.

CARD GAMES. A good hostess sees to it that those gainfully employed at her card tables should be as nearly financially and competently level as possible. A bridge four should not consist of Mr Ely Culbertson, a member of White's Club and two destitute ladies who have not yet learnt Contract. By the same token it is wrong to involve the impecunious young in a game of poker with the horribly cunning and revoltingly rich old. It is true that the hardened poker players prefer to stake more than they can afford, but as an after dinner amusement, and one, what is more, that is forced upon him, it is not particularly alluring for the unwilling guest to find himself betting fivers simply so as not to look unco-operative. As it is certainly not etiquette to ask a guest whether he can afford the stakes suggested, it is essential that a hostess discovers this beforehand, either by subtle investigation into his *modus vivendi*, or, more simply, by asking someone. In most cases she will already be aware of his worth, but the odd young man met yesterday at a cocktail party is sometimes difficult to assess. The kindest thing is to suppose he is poor until he mentions his yacht, when it is not only possible to treble the stakes but also to ask him whether he would be interested in a theatrical project she has in mind.

Bridge is supposed to be a game played for pleasure by friendly people, but it is the only game, save American football, in which acrimony is allowed without infringing the bounds of good taste, and for which it is permissible to practise beforehand facial contortions suitable for unnerving one's opponents. Sarcasm, tongue-clicking and honest-to-goodness blood rows are perfectly in order, and if ladies can burst into tears so much the better.

Only the other day a woman of exquisite beauty, beloved by all and possessing perfect health and a summer ermine coat, was fished from the river in a moribund condition. Saved from a watery grave she lay for weeks in a delirium, able only to repeat again and again in a heart-breaking voice, "Oh God, I should have played the knave!" She is nearly re-covered now, but her physicians still only allow her to play Beggar my Neighbour with packs of cards in which the knaves have been replaced by jokers. It is doubtful whether the poor creature will ever be well enough to play Bridge again. She is, of course, an ex-treme case, but on the whole it can be said that the Bridge World is riddled with neuroses and is prone to bouts of irritability, insomnia and depression.

For this reason Family Bridge, particularly if it is of an instructional nature, should only be played for half an hour at a time, the exasperated parents coaxing their sullen offspring with as much self-control as possible and refraining from deploring out loud that it is the greatest pity they have given birth to morons. Children should reflect before they hurl their cards on to the floor and stamp out of the room, because if they want to play Bridge they must *learn* how to play it. It is not a thing one can pick up in a casual manner, like rummy; nor can it be played by the light of nature, reason or guesswork, although the latter may prove helpful at times. Few people, left on their own, would assume that a fistful of Hearts calls for a bid of One Club, unless, that is, they were mad, but under proper guidance they will learn *le dessous des cartes*, which is a mystery divulged only to those who strain and strive.

An inexperienced Bridge player occasionally wins a rubber by playing his cards in such a peculiar order his opponents become bewildered. So amazed are they that he has not played the Queen of Spades when they expected him to (it is *de rigueur* to know exactly where every card in the pack is residing) they begin to wonder whether they have not missed it after all, or else they suspect something outstandingly canny, some finesse they have never heard of; but after a little while the novice may find that they have caught on to his system of playing his cards in strict numerical rotation, and they will deal with him as he has shuffled with them.

In the very highest Bridge circles it is not necessary actually to play the cards at all. After each player has mentioned the suit of which he has none, the player next the dealer puts down the seven of clubs or the five of diamonds, and then the player to his left puts *all* his cards on the table and says, "I think the rest are mine?". The tyro should on no account attempt this sort of thing until he has been hard at it for at least a decade, for though he will *think* the rest are his he will not be *sure*, and there is nothing so disagreeable as to be caught counting your tricks before they are hatched.

If it pleases you to watch other people playing Patience, see to it that you watch in silence and without wincing. A bite from a malaria mosquito is not half as maddening to a Patience player as the remark, "Look, darling, the red seven on the black eight!" A hissing, smothered whistle of alarm when the player, speeding through the pack in an agony of nerves covers the ace of spades, is enough to drive the most rational insane.

CROSSWORDS. Before embarking on communal puzzle-solving it is well to be *au courant* with the minds of your assistants. Thus you can apportion the clues with the minimum explanation and the maximum hope. It is etiquette to give the literal minded or the slightly deaf all the anagrams, handing them a pencil and a piece of paper and forgetting all about them. It is kinder to remember to inform them, however, when you have absent-mindedly worked out the anagrams for yourself, as there is something rather pathetic about people labouring when the labour is o'er.

The man who holds the newspaper is always at an advantage, so it is polite to offer it to the senior member of the group regardless of whether he or she can read.

Quotations are almost always solved by the process of elimination or else by divine inspiration, as nearly everybody remembers the bit that comes before and the bit that comes after, but the bit required stays paralysed on the tips of their tongues. If only nobody had mentioned it they could have recited the whole thing with ease, of course.

Patience should be exercised in dealing with those who are unaware of a crossword compiler's tortuous mind. Although you know that "It occurs in a quaint old Spanish custom" in four letters is either aqua, into, told or anis, you *must* permit your aunt to recall the visit she made to Madrid in 1910 and allow her to cudgel her brains in search of some local customs that were both quaint and old. The eventual explanation as to why the answer is aqua can be exceedingly tedious, but affection demands much that is fatiguing. Another challenge to patience comes from those whose mental processes are so profound as to be unfathomable. Say that you give them a word of five letters signifying "something more". They will think deeply—you can see them doing it, looking over their glasses into space or chewing their thumb nails—and then suddenly a

look of revelation transfigures their faces and they say,
"Do you think it could be hypodermic, dear?" It is
useless to enquire where their minds have journeyed
since last they spoke or whether they encountered
Doctor Freud in their travels, for they are often,
strangely enough, the least complicated of your acquaintances and very simple, dear people. So do you
be simple and dear too, and merely point out the diver-
gence between the number of letters required and
those offered.

Crossword puzzles are excellent sedatives and
should be administered to all especially nerve-
wracked cases. Those about to become fathers and
those about to become brides are particularly susceptible to their drugging influence, as are also those
waiting for bad news, good news, or even THE news.

CHAPTER XIV

MANNERS AND MODES

May every tea-time be accursed,
May honey spill and éclairs burst,
And may those ladies die of thirst
Who dare to put the milk in first!

THE STANDARD set by our parents regarding the use of words has been lowered to such a degree it can almost be said to be furled. Words, like fashions, disappear and recur throughout English history, and one generation's phraseology, while it may seem abominably second-rate to the next, becomes first-rate to the third; but our forebears would not or could not take this matter lightly. Any man who said, "I'm going up to town to see a show" was not only not a gentleman but was automatically denied every human virtue and grace. It was unthinkable that he could be kind, wise or intelligent, and if one had been foolish enough to suppose, for a brief second, that he was quite an entertaining fellow one was immediately shocked out of such nonsense by hearing such a frightful remark issuing from his caddish lips. Even the most passionate love curled up and died at the word "serviette", yes, though it were spoken by Adonis himself with the tenderness of a bruise; and an invitation to a "week-end" or a "ring on the 'phone" met with an instinctive rebuff. It was hardly credible that there existed people vile enough to call their children "kids", or so debased they said "pardon" when they hiccoughed. They were beyond the pale. Untouchables. The élite retired behind their iron curtain and continued "going to the play" when they "came up to London", while their children wiped their mouths on "napkins" and went away "from Saturday to Monday" and said "Forgive me" or "I'm so sorry" when they scrambled over people in the stalls.

Nowadays, although of course it is not possible to *love* people who use serviettes, napkin users can like them very much indeed, and can even, if they are sufficiently rich, accept their hospitality. It is still painful to have friends who "live in town", but they can always point out that their grandparents did, so why in the hell shouldn't they, and it is abominably hard to find an answer. The present social revolution has so thoroughly confused things one is almost obliged to like people for their good qualities rather than for their English, for now that Earls live in Edgware and Baronets in basements anything goes. It is a very great tragedy to snub a man because he cannot pronounce Marjoribanks and then discover he is the third son of a Duke.

It is rash, too, to deplore the use of fish knives, educated though you may be in the two-forks or one-and-a-toast-pusher school, for many a noble house has used up all its spare forks trying to open sardine tins, and is left with exactly six, rather blue at the prongs. It has also been discovered that a fish knife is a considerable aid to the eating of fish, but that, of course, is beside the point.

Neither in the matter of clothes can a man be judged by the old standards, so do not be so foolish as to suppose that the gentleman strolling down Bond Street in the well-fitting grey pin-striped suit and the soft-as-the-breath-of-a-dove suède shoes is a Guards' officer on his way to Cartier. He is not. He is a German refugee on his way to the Ritz. The seedy individual in the corduroy bags shuffling along behind him is Sir Simon Wivelscombe going to the Treasury, and there, wearing a blue coat over brown trousers, is Lord Fitzraine on his way to Lyons' Corner House. It is just a matter of adjustment. Everything is the same save that the balance of flannel and suède has been shifted.

Ladies are equally hard to identify these days for they can no longer afford British national costumes which, as everybody knows, consist of blue and white flowered crêpe-de-chine dresses in summer and black coats and skirts in winter; but they can most easily be recognised by their hands, which are roughened by housework, and, of course, by their chins which *still* are not there. On the whole it is advisable to be nice to everyone at the *start*; to men who look like sanitary inspectors and sometimes are sanitary inspectors; to women who look like prostitutes; to prostitutes who look like Old Roedean girls, and to jockeys wearing Old Harrovian ties, for it is impossible to tell in what disguise the aristocracy may now be lurking, and many a *gaffe* has been made by jumping too hastily to conclusions.

ASSUMPTIONS. Although you doubtless revolve in the highest circles, it is an error of taste to take it for granted that the person with whom you are conversing is bound to know the names of all the stately homes of England, or supposing he does, can remember the names of the people who live inside them. If, going on the basis that the landed gentry are inevitably on intimate terms, you say, "The most amazing thing happened when I was staying at Bosfiddle. After luncheon—Bridget, of course, was making one of those ineffably boring chair seats which, as you know, sprinkle the whole house—and the rest of us were half asleep, when a pheasant flew right through the window and settled on the chandelier! Poor Eddie . . . etc."; however amazing this story may be and with whatever verve you may tell it, if your listener can't remember whom Bosfiddle belongs to he will cease paying attention quite early on. Although his eye may be fixed politely on you, behind it will be a mind so busily ticking off Dukes and endeavouring to seat them in their appropriate seats that, as far as your story is concerned, you will have, as is said in vulgar parlance, had it.

That you should assume that any friend of yours *must* know that Bosfiddle belongs to Lord Cadwallader is doubtless very flattering, in theory that is, but in practice a man who is ignorant of this blatantly obvious fact labours under a severe strain. For unless he is bold enough to enquire *right at the beginning* who is the rightful owner of this noble mansion, there comes a moment when it is too late to ask. This moment cannot be computed in terms of hours or minutes, but it comes, it comes, as surely as death.

Therefore, even if it is not etiquette, it is kind to mention the names of people before you mention their houses, and in so doing to avoid calling them solely by their Christian names. The Christian names of people

G

one does not know, particularly if they are peers, are at best uninteresting and, at worst, imbue the stranger with a sense of loneliness and social desolation. Be extremely careful too, not to imagine you know people better than you do, for if, on the strength of one weekend, you persist in talking about Lord Cumberland as "dear old Freddie" there will come a time when, brought face to face with this dear old friend of yours, it becomes apparent that Lord Cumberland, like all aristocrats, is so weak in the head he fails even to recognise you.

The stage, of course, is a different matter. It is indeed usual to call Mr Noel Coward Noel long before you meet him, and for the rest of the cast, as it were, it is perfectly correct to assume that they are all in some way connected with the Darling family.

THE RICH. In dealing with the very rich it is well to remember that though generous to a fault in all big matters they tend to be mean in small, so scrupulous care should be taken to pay for any stamps acquired or telephone calls made while in their houses. It will also be observed that when they offer you lifts in their cars these will only be *as far as Marble Arch*, and never to your front door. It is not etiquette to remark on these idiosyncrasies, but to accept them, along with emerald brooches, with proper expressions of gratitude. As Dr

Johnson so sagaciously observed, "Smile with the wise and feed with the rich".

THE AGED. It is etiquette to be courteous to the aged, however offensive or tiresome they may be, and though they may slander your friends, dismiss your servants and beat your children with hard malacca canes, no word of censure must be permitted to pass your lips. The reward for this unnatural restraint comes when you yourself reach the age of indiscretion; the age when you no longer fear the censure of others or care a hoot in hell for their opinions; when being kind is no longer a matter of expediency or are manners the stepping-stones to success. On that joyful day when you realise that you are too old to worry about anything except the next meal, you in your turn can cast off the trappings of polite society and be free to express the sentiments you so patiently dammed when you were younger.

In order not to rob the aged of these long-awaited pleasures it is kinder not to assume that they are mentally deficient or decrepit. Although theoretically it is etiquette to wait upon them hand and foot, to heave them out of chairs and pick up their glasses when they drop them, in practice the old prefer to have to *ask* you to help them should they desire to be helped, thereby implying you are extremely thoughtless and don't care whether they break their necks or not. This is much more fun for them. They *like* saying, "Shut the window, dear, you know I can't stand a draught!", and it is a cruel disappointment to them if you remember to keep it closed. It is a moot point, of course, whether it is more fun to be assisted from a chair and to say crossly, "Thank you, but I'm not paralysed *yet*!" or to be left struggling until one is forced to cry "Joan, I really *do* think you might help me!" Both systems have their advocates.

Try not to be irritated with the aged because they have not heard of Bing Crosby. Quite early on in life the mind refuses to absorb any more names of dance tunes, and as the years progress it rejects the names of film stars, crooners, cricketers, race horses and wireless comedians in ever increasing numbers. You may not be aware of it, but there is a generation just behind you, already treading on your heels in their great brogues, who are already irritated with *you* for never having heard of Rose Murphy. (Well, have you?)

Dependent on the way they have shaped their lives the aged are either delightfully cynical or completely starry-eyed; either caustic or compassionate; disillusioned or eternally hopeful; bitter or benevolent. As examples of their particular philosophies they can teach you much, and many a truth has been apprehended for the first time at a grandmother's knee; but while seeking advice from those of advanced years see to it that you keep to fundamental problems, problems that have puzzled the cosmos since its initial launch into space. Asking your grandmother whether she thinks you should do your hair like Lana Turner is a sheer waste of breath.

MANNERS. Until you have known people a long, long time do not poke their fires, switch on their radios, open their windows, close them, rearrange their flowers, take their stamps or slap their babies *without first asking permission*.

A hostess's generous but nevertheless automatic suggestion that you should make yourself at home and do exactly as you like must be countered with a resolve to do nothing of the silly sort. She does not mean it for one single minute. It is a LIE. Any word or gesture that is even faintly possessive should be avoided like the plague, for to find a guest crouching before her fire holding a poker guiltily in her hand, or to catch her struggling secretly with a window, sends the blood rushing in angry, thumping waves to a hostess's head. Nobody quite knows why this is save that presumption is a sin in others and the fire was going splendidly anyway.

Gentlemen always rise to their feet when ladies enter a room unless (*a*) the ladies are their wives, in which case they only rise when anybody is looking, (*b*) the ladies are particularly restless. In the latter event, when a lady has left and re-entered a room three times in the space of a quarter of an hour, she should not expect a gentleman to do more than raise his spine an inch or so from his chair, and if he is feigning sleep she must be indulgent.

In society it is etiquette for ladies to have the best chairs and get handed things. In the home the reverse is the case. That is why ladies are more sociable than gentlemen.

When somebody mispronounces a word, do not pronounce it correctly a minute afterwards. This calls for almost superhuman control, but at least five minutes should be allowed to elapse between the *gaffe* and the humiliation.

HOLINESS. On encountering people dressed for Church on Sunday morning it is etiquette to do all in one's power to prevent them getting there. Various bribes, such as drives in the country, walks in the Park or a nice cosy gossip by the fire should immediately be extended in seductive terms. Virtue in others, in fact, is always to be deplored and not only church-goers but also those setting out for East End Clubs or Charity Committee Meetings should be waylaid. By the same token those who do not drink should be pressed repeatedly to take of the fruit of the vine "for the stomach's sake" if for nobody else's. Because it is uncomfortable to be irreligious, irresponsible, and slightly drunk when surrounded by the ostentatiously pure, it is worth while spending ages in decoying them from off the path of righteousness, and a lady has, on such occasions, golden opportunity for testing her persuasive powers. Unfortunately she can but rarely test them out on gentlemen, as so many of these are unbelievably evil already, but she can sometimes charm them away from duty dinners and can nearly always prevent them from taking their mothers to concerts at the Wigmore Hall. At any rate she should try.

STORIES. In telling a funny story be sure you remember the *point* of the story before you begin. Know your audience. To embark on a tale, however humorous, concerning racial or religious characteristics and then to realise half way through that you are telling it to a Roman Catholic Jewess is to know true suffering. The mind whizzes round like a squirrel in a cage seeking to find some loop-hole of escape, and many a lady has been forced to turn her hero into a Mahommedan Portuguese or a Christianly Scientific Mongolian, thereby saving her face but losing considerably on the applause.

If a story is coarse, let it, please, be funny.

When listening to a story if, after the first few sentences, you realise you have heard it before *say so* unless it is being told by a near relative, in which case you will have already heard it so many times once more won't matter. All good husbands and wives laugh like hyenas at each other's tales and even hand out "feed" lines to get the stories going.

DINING OUT. Dining out these days should be undertaken with alertness. The domestic situation must be swiftly appraised so that no embarrassing gaffes are made. If there is a withered Latvian in a dirty apron hovering in the corner of the dining-room do NOT start absentmindedly stacking your hostess's plates. If there are no slaves in sight scrape back your chair an inch or two between each course, this being a recognised signal for your host to say "Oh no, please! Stay right where you are! My wife will do it!"

If the food is placed on the sideboard it is advisable that not more than seven out of eight people should attempt to serve one another at the same time.

It is polite, at some juncture, to raise one of your hostess's plates above your head, preferably before the snoek has been laid upon it, so as to observe the mark of the china embossed on its bottom. This is a very flattering thing to do and it is of small moment whether you see anything there or not or, seeing it, know what it signifies.

As at most modern dinner parties there is never a moment when all the guests are sitting down together, there is none of that awkwardness about knowing when to turn, conversationally, from one neighbour to the other. In the old days there was a definite feeling of suspense after the *canards aux navets*, a subconscious current that prevented one from embarking on anything too profound at this point. All views on the Trinity or Tolstoi had to be aired and folded away by the third from last mouthful of *sauce piquante*, for in a moment or two one's hostess would turn from Sir Evelyn Bogg, with whom she had been conversing on Time and the Stars, to say to Mr Flummeroy-Smith, "Well, and how's the fishing?" This *volte face*, designed to be infectious, then spread slowly down the table, getting jammed at Milly Fitzjohn's girl, who was so entangled talking about the weather to Captain Boycott she could in no wise unloose herself, and leaving poor old Mr de Crespigny staring, with an interest worthy of better literature, at the menu. These hazards now are past, and dinner conversation is largely confined to cross-talk between females abandoned at the table, punctuated by male enquiries from the sideboard as to whether they want potatoes.

Except in intimate circles it is not done to point out to your husband in ringing tones that he has a blob of spinach on his chin and will he please remove it? The etiquette on this parlous occasion is to catch his eye—and the eyes of wives are notoriously magnetic—and then wipe your own chin on your napkin, if needs be until it is raw. Even if you do not take the skin off you will remove the powder, but unless your husband is particularly dim-witted this manoeuvre will also be the means of removing any superfluous vegetable matter that may be clinging to him. Some husbands, seeing that their helpmeets are endeavouring to convey some sort of message but wholly incapable of guessing its import, spoil the whole thing by pausing in their conversation with their neighbours to ask what in the hell does Blanche think she's doing? The answer to this is "Nothing, dear", for a wife should be the last person to draw attention to her husband's ineptitude with a knife and fork.

Tentative offers to wash up after a meal should always be made unless it is quite obvious there are servants around. Remember that when you offer to wash up you really mean dry down, as it is the prerogative of hostesses to plunge their hands into greasy water and the privilege of guests to endeavour to wipe the remains of the grease off the plates with a rather damp dishcloth.

Do not, in excess of zeal, put the crockery and cutlery away, working on the basis that the china will go in the china cupboard and the knives with the other knives, for this is never so. A good housekeeper is as full of whimsies as Mary Rose and likely as not she has thought up a perfectly good reason why the mustard pots should live in the bread bin and the coffee cups with the boot polish, although she may not, on the spur of the moment, be able to tell you what it is. So when you have dried, leave well alone.

Gentlemen tend to be humorous when drying up and are apt to recollect tricks with wine glasses, so, although the steadier members of the sex can be useful in rather a scrappy way, in cases where the gentlemen's temperaments are not known, it is more practical to suggest they go away. They will like doing this very much indeed.

NEVER talk Shop.

When you stand up and say "Well, I'm afraid I must go now", GO.

FRIENDSHIP. When a lady is giving an evening party she has the right to expect the fullest co-operation from her immediate friends, which means that they should circulate among the less favoured guests and assist, by plying them with drink and clean, cultured conversation, in their entertainment. Friendship also has its etiquette, and this is widely breached when six of a lady's most intimate friends, all of whom have seen each other already three times that week, disappear into another room and hold a party of their own. Cliques, by which are meant small groups of people who telephone to one another every morning, talking in a very special private language in which most of the consonants are missing, are absolutely delightful except at a party, when they are absolutely not.

THE VELVET GLOVE. However much you may dislike another lady you should conceal your dislike under a cloak of *bonhomie*. There is no reason why you should not from time to time produce a rapier from out its folds with which to prod her in a vulnerable spot, but see that it is a rapier and not a bludgeon. No gentlewoman should resort to rude words, nor should she ever slash another lady across the face with a piece of toast; rather should she lay little verbal time bombs, so heavily disguised in smiles that the enemy is unaware she is in the midst of them until they explode. This may be several hours later when she is in her bath.

For some reason—it is believed to be something to do with men—ladies are hypersensitive about the passing years. It seems they pass too quickly and are apt to take ladies along with them, printing upon their faces as they go all but indelible stigmata of their passage.

As somebody—probably St Paul—said, "The flesh is the *devil*!" and in order to exorcise it ladies go to great trouble and expense. That age is a delicate matter even Governments dare not deny, and on no buff forms or questionnaires is a lady asked to put her age if she is above fifty. "Just put 'Over 50' " they say. In implying, therefore, that a lady is not as young as she pretends, an ill-wisher can inject a subtle poison into her hardening arteries. "And how old is your eldest, dear?" is a very aggravating remark. Or, charmingly: "Was the Great Exhibition at *all* like Wembley?". Or to a query: "Well I really haven't the faintest idea—I mean, I don't think I was born then, was I?". Or again: "It must be strange seeing all the old fashions coming round again! I expect you wish to heaven you'd kept your old *guêpieres*, don't you?" or, "Somehow, I never can remember you're a granny now!"

H O U S E S . A lady should at all times and under every circumstance admire the houses, gardens, children and dogs of others, however ghastly these may be. Truthfulness and good manners have never made congenial bedfellows, but though there are some who prize truth above all the virtues there are considerably more who prefer to deny it in the name of charity. It is also, let us be frank, much less trouble to be nice. By all means discuss the pros and cons of terra-cotta wallpapers and green shadow chintzes while your friends are still strewing their rooms with *samples*, but once the walls are deeply painted with chocolate and the chairs fulsomely covered with violet gabardine, admire. Pronounce the whole thing absolutely wizard. It is well to be particularly cautious when visiting a friend who is in the throes of re-decorating her home. There was once a lady not a million miles from here, who walked smartly into a dining-room crying "Angela! What fun you're going to have doing *this* up!" only to discover that the renovation had been completed the week before. The incident can only be described as ugly.

Do not say any of the following:

(*a*) What a pity you installed a gas cooker; electricity is so much cheaper.

(*b*) What a pity you installed an electric cooker, gas is so much cheaper.

(*c*) What a pity you didn't think of having anthracite; it heats the water so much better than coke and lasts so much longer.

(*d*) It is a curious thing but we always seem to get all the fuel we need.

(*e*) There is a marvellous new stuff called activated crunch, but of course you wouldn't be able to use it as it comes in blocks six feet by four and has to be broken up with a drill.

(*f*) Yes, we have central heating throughout the whole house.

(*g*) You should have an immersion heater.

(*h*) I'm afraid you'll be thoroughly disappointed with your immersion heater.

(*i*) Oh but, darling, how could you? Those contraptions explode all the time!

GARDENS. Miss Ruth Draper has made garden owners extremely sensitive about showing them to visitors, and there is probably not one single horticulturist left in England who dares to say "You should have seen these last week!" without parenthesising the words or making some reference to the distinguished *diseuse*. The fact remains that nearly every garden a lady visits *did* look better the week before, and were this not a common mystery shared by the whole human race she might be inclined to think her presence radiates some awful blight, some poisonous vapour which causes Canterbury bells to shrivel and roses to curl their petals at her approach. Nevertheless, though a lady or, for that matter, a gentleman may never see a garden at the height of its beauty, this being reserved for days when its owners are alone, what they do see they must applaud. Confronted by four snapdragons and a distraught-looking clump of

Michaelmas daisies it can be remembered with benefit to the soul of the observer that "the meanest flower
that blows can give, Thoughts that do often lie too
deep for tears". What these thoughts are exactly can
be worked out later on, but at the time it is merely
necessary to comment on the quality of the blooms in
default of the quantity. For the non-gardening visitor
a garden pricked with a few flowers should not be an
insuperable problem, but unfortunately the higher,
more intellectual type of horticulturist tends to go in
solely for shrubs around whose apparently lifeless
twigs hang labels instead of leaves. Brought at great
expense from the Himalayas or Peru, sheltered by
large bamboo screens, and visited daily by anxious
nurserymen, these plants offer no aid to the visitor.
After gazing in awe at the moribund exiles, the sodden
roots of which are struggling long and lone in the cloy-
ing English clay, there is very little else to do. Only
ladies imaginative to the point of insanity can go into
raptures over a dead stick. All the same those who have
placed such faith in it should be encouraged, for when
in two years' time the wizened thing puts forth a
dozen microscopic flowers, which the Spring will immediately nip between callous fingers, they will remember the friend who too believed and understood
and was kind. They may even send her a vegetable
marrow as a token of gratitude.

CHILDREN. A little of other people's children goes a very long way, but however far it goes it must be followed with a loving eye. No lady, even though she be provoked beyond endurance, should allow the word "don't" to pass her lips in front of another's child unless, of course, the child's parents happen to be out of the room, when she can, and indeed should, abuse it with impunity. Early morning visits heralding games in bed, practical jokes involving a lot of water, a constant demand for attention, tantrums, tears and the throwing about of custard at mealtimes must be endured with unflinching *sang froid*—in fact *sang froid* is barely sufficient. Rather should it be stated, or at any rate implied, that there is nothing so adorable as a child's wilful little ways, and anything like a tiddler in the teapot or salt in the sugar should be welcomed as a delightful sign of precocity.

Sometimes a lady is left alone for at least ten minutes with a reasonably large baby; one that can fall off the sofa but cannot get back on to it again, has not the strength to stand yet can, with one fine careless gesture, sweep all the ornaments off a table, and is of the correct proportions to crawl under every piece of furniture in the room and bump its head on it on the way out. Etiquette demands that this creature should be kept in a state of subjection until its mother returns, and also, which is more difficult, should be so enter-

H

tained it is unaware its mother has temporarily abandoned it. Distractions such as watches, lipsticks and
strings of pearls are now very old-fashioned, and no
baby worthy of the name will stick them for a second.
The knobs of a wireless set are fairly good and the
knobs of a television one even better, but failing these
the spoken word, if it is unfamiliar enough, has a re-
markably hypnotic effect. Stare the child full in its
china blue eyes and say, "You sinful morsel of animated matter, reclining with such indecent abandon
on this *chaise longue* purchased by your father at a Sale
in Kidderminster in 1945, are you aware that you are
largely composed of water and that there is not much
difference between you and a cucumber?" Do not
wait for a reply, but hasten on to one of Burke's
speeches, and in ringing tones proclaim "Corrupt influence, which is in itself the perennial spring of all
prodigality, and of all disorder; which loads more
than millions of debt; which takes away vigour from
our arms, wisdom from our councils, and every
shadow of authority and credit from the most vener-
able parts of our constitution, etc., etc.". Again, without pausing for breath, for any break in the narrative
thread is fatal, cry, "My child, it may come as a complete surprise to you, but after much investigation it
has been definitely proved by an eminent historian
called Wilberforce Stodge, that the cakes King Alfred

so negligently burned were not cakes at all, but buns, and that from this mishap is derived the term Hot Cross Buns. This may not interest you, of course, so much as your toes, but in future years, when your toes are not so liberally flavoured with violet talcum powder you may find the aforementioned buns considerably more palatable". And then on! on!

The great thing is to *sustain* this monologue, for if you falter for an instant that mesmerised face lifted with such terrified wonder to yours may suddenly crumple like a burst balloon, turn crimson, and hurl itself downwards on to a cushion in paroxysms of grief. Mothers who return to find their children upside down and in hysterics are considerably flattered, of course, but they cannot disguise their contempt for the baby-sitters. As for the latter, they are mortified beyond words, although this does not prevent them from relating at great length how it all came about, and how they're most frightfully sorry but they really didn't do a thing except pull a few funny faces.

DOGS. Entertaining the temporarily forsaken dog is another affair altogether, and it is doubtful whether a recital of Burke's Speeches or, for that matter, Burke's Peerage will be sufficiently distracting, even if declaimed on all fours. Stroking the ears and scratching the stomach are fairly diverting, and cries of "Rabbits?" or "Walkies?" promote a brief interest, but in the end it is better, or at any rate easier, to let a dog concentrate on its grief and permit it to sit whimpering and shivering by the door, a picture of misery. Really, it prefers it this way.

MATRIMONY. It sometimes happens that ladies' daughters become engaged to Rumanian acrobats, and their sons to ambitious strip-tease artistes, and this upsets ladies very much indeed, as they always had in mind quite different types of helpmeets for their children—young shoots from ancient family trees or the rich and handsome offspring of industrial magnates, or even the flowers of the aristocracy (although this entails a life of such drudgery only the most snobbish parent would wish for such a thing). All being fair in love and war it is all right for a lady to attempt, with all the weapons she has at her disposal, to break up, smash and otherwise pulverise any romantic attachments of which she disapproves, and to take no account whatsoever of love. She need not deny that such a thing exists, but at any rate she can vigorously affirm that it does not last, not at least unless it is tended. She feels perfectly certain that after a few years of connubial bliss her daughter will find the weight of her love for her Rumanian acrobat is by no means balanced by the appalling tedium of pursuing

him, in tights, on to the stage of every Variety Hall in
the world, there to place on his revolving air-borne
legs several revolving hoops, there to hand him a
silken handkerchief with which to dry his hands. She
is equally sure that in due course her son's strip-teaser
will get the "call" again to resume her profession and
will once more yearn to take the veil or, to be more precise, the seven veils, with a view to removing them at
leisure to an enthralled public. And she does not think
her son will like it. Therefore let there be fuss, let
there be threats, let there be tears or, if a lady is courageous enough, let there be just the opposite, for such
is the perverseness of human nature if two people are
thrown together hard and often, if the offending parties are invited to stay for weeks and surrounded by
gushing kindness and heaps of boring relatives they
tend to become more aware of their differences and
less aware of their burning love.

Nevertheless there are burning loves that can con-
sume all hazards in their paths, and when a lady sees
that her daughter is adamantly resolved to marry the
stoker on the 9.15 to Carlisle and that nothing she can
say or do will stop her, then let her give in gracefully.
Grace is a virtue which a lady would be wise to hold on
to. Let it go for a moment and she becomes a woman,
which, as any woman will tell you, is a very depressing
thing to be. Thus shall a lady, the last bridge burned,

the last raft sunk, go down with colours flying and take into her arms the stoker with his dear, black face. Let her pronounce him, loudly, from every convenient housetop, to be an absolute treasure, and let there be no nonsense about going to bed with 'flu on the day of the wedding, no words of recrimination, no tearful warnings, and no sobbing on the bosoms of talkative friends. The courageous acceptance of inevitable disaster is always becoming, particularly when the two main tragedians are quite certain the disaster is delightful.

P R A I S E . Such is the possessiveness of human beings, it is extraordinarily difficult for them to disassociate themselves from the triumphs of their nearest and dearest, and it is usual to accept praise for a loved one with the same embarrassed repudiation one would employ were it offered to oneself. Should someone pass a remark to the effect that a lady's husband is the best-looking man this side of heaven she must on no account say, "Yes, *isn't* he?" Rather should she blush, look down her nose (or, of course, if it is *retroussé*, up it), twist her handkerchief, wriggle her toes, and then mumble, very awkwardly, "Oh, do you really think so?". Be her husband the uncrowned king of his profession, talented, brilliant, renowned and wonderful in all his ways, a wife must acknowledge each tribute to his fame with a deprecatory smile as though to say, "It may be so but it would be dreadfully conceited of me to agree with you". A lady should be under the impression that she made her husband with her own two hands, and indeed all her family's successes should be considered the result of personal labour, to be applauded in secret but only modestly acclaimed in public.

"Yes, he's really doing quite well. He got a First at Oxford, which was rather lucky."

"Harold's book? Oh, how sweet of you! Yes, it is quite a success. Over a million copies I believe . . . something like that anyway. . . ."

"I know I oughtn't to boast, but James has been given the Nobel Prize!" may be taken as examples of how a lady can gracefully accept compliments for her dear ones without completely renouncing her own mythical share in their prowess. The moment a lady affirms without a trace of shyness that her husband is a superb painter, a brilliant psychologist, a marvellous mechanic, an unsurpassed dentist or a perfect plumber you may be sure that the lady no longer loves him.

BAD HABITS. Upon reaching the age of sixty-five ladies should see to it that those nearest and dearest to them present them with a list of their bad habits. Although it will probably be too late to mend any of

them, at least they will have the satisfaction of knowing why it is that for so many years their grandchildren
have, on certain occasions, flung themselves off their
chairs in paroxysms of mirth, and why their friends
have often seemed so unnaturally fretful.

It is the ignorance of the exact nature of their bad
habits that makes the latter days of the aged so extraordinarily tragic, for though they may be aware there
is something the matter with them it seems nobody
cares enough or dares enough to tell them what it is.
Even though they ask they will not be told. Respect
for those of riper years, however imbecile, is so en-
grained in the human mind that it requires a stupen-
dous effort for a lady to tell her bachelor uncle that his
habit of sniffing is driving all his relatives and friends
mad. It is, however, a deed that should be done, not
only once, but many times, so that the very phrase
"Darling, *don't* sniff!" becomes a bad habit in itself.

There was once a charming woman who was much
given to brooding on the mutability of earthly great-
ness. During these meditative spells she, like the ru-
minant cow, chewed things. In the space of a few
months she ate her way through two silver paper cut-
ters (only losing heart when she reached the knobs at
the ends), three pairs of tortoiseshell spectacles and
dozens of knitting needles. Then, of course, being unable to cut the pages of a book, being sightless and

without any knitting, she grew extremely restless, then neurotic, then demented. She left her husband and children, sold all her investments, with the proceeds of which she bought seventeen crates full of lead pencils, and retired to a lodging-house at West Wittering to chew them. The responsibility for this tragedy rested upon her family, no member of whom had had the kindness or the good sense to remove the first, or at any rate the second, paper cutter from between her molars.

It is, of course, a moot point whether anybody listens to anything anybody else says, but in some cases it is possible, by constant reiteration, to scratch the mind's surface and insert a few barbs. But this should be done when the mind is still flexible. It should not be left too late. A lady therefore, who is approaching the prime of life, should ask her husband or children to stand guard over her idiosyncrasies. Let her immediately be informed should she hum too much or nervously twist her handkerchief. Should she have taken to a wig let her dear ones tell her the moment they see her levering it up with a pencil, and when her teeth are no longer joined on to her gums let someone be swift to remind her that *rateliers* should be worn inside the mouth and, whenever possible, be kept stationary. Even though a lady does nothing about it, it is pleasant to *know*. Knowledge is power, and it is nice for her to

realise she has the wherewithal to exasperate or enter-
tain. After all, to annoy their contemporaries and de-
light the young are two of the few pleasures left to old
age, and a *toupet* set at a jaunty angle, an indelicate
blow on the soup, gloves worn at luncheon and a
twitching eye may achieve in an hour what might
otherwise take days to accomplish.

SECRETS. It is etiquette for groups of friends to have
secrets the secrecy for which is not always patently obvious, and a lady should enter thoroughly into the
spirit of the thing and do her level best to maintain
that aura of mystery which surrounds her dear ones'
doings, even if she cannot for the life of her see the
reason for it. In the literary and theatrical world the
mania for secrets is largely due to the vulpine machina-
tions of other members of the profession, whose
jealous natures seize and tear apart the still unsigned
contract and whose tongues flay the written word long
before it is written. There is also a strong element of
superstition which prevents, say, an author from
divulging the form of his work in hand just in case,
having told everyone he is writing a book on Fundamental Feudalism, it turns into a novel. There is a love
of the dramatic too, which makes people assume a
cloak and dagger appearance at the smallest opportunity.

A lady should always try very hard to keep a secret although it is admittedly perfectly maddening to discover, after a passage of time, that it has long ceased to be one. By the same token she should try to remember the lies she has told for her friends, the lunches she is supposed to have given them, the nights their spirits, if not their bodies, have lain in her beds, and all the prevaricating complications of prompted telephone conversations. The friends of friends in common with the plans of friends are extraordinarily difficult to follow, but every attempt should be made to appear interested in both.

It can therefore be taken for granted, as is the air daily inhaled into the lungs, that although Dick is composing the most beautiful music, nobody must know what it is for; that although Joyce is going into a play nobody must know which play; that although Susan is engaged, nobody must know who to; that although Winifred is soon coming back from America, nobody must know the exact date she lands. These secrets if divulged, would so rock the world no lady in her senses would dare to take the risk.

DISSEMBLING. Sometimes, indeed quite often, a lady finds herself in conversation with a gentleman who appears to have read, seen, heard, done and been everything that she hasn't, and there is no doubt at all that a lady gets tired of saying, "No, as a matter of fact I haven't!". It is then, more out of pique than perjury, she may suddenly say, "Yes, as a matter of fact I have".

There is something rather invigorating in arguing about a book one has not read or in criticising a film one has not seen, but it is wise—and not only wise but essential—to know just the tiniest bit about them; to have glanced at reviews in the papers or to have heard them discussed. The pits into which the unwary can fall are obvious, but there are many, alas, which even the most astute cannot avoid. One such is when a gentleman recollects for a lady's benefit a scene in the book *Woe for the Moon* in which the author describes a fight by two men in a cave full of bats, and after she has agreed it was superb and added a word about the atmosphere and another word about some stalactites she has invented, after, in fact, she has thoroughly committed herself, he remembers the bat scene came in quite a *different* book—something called *I was a Troglodyte*, which is so far only published in America. The etiquette for a lady in this instance is to change the subject as quickly as possible, the most time-honoured ways of achieving this change being to knock over a glass or have a choking fit.

On the whole, and providing one is in good spirits and feeling reasonably bright, it is not hard to con-

verse for a short space of time on subjects about which
one knows little, and it is indeed often amusing to see
how cunningly one can steer the conversational
barque, hoisting and lowering her sails, tacking this
way and that to avoid reefs, and finally racing fever-
ishly for home with the outboard engine making a
loud and cheerful noise. To converse on subjects
about which one knows NOTHING, however, should
be avoided. Economics and racing are two subjects
about which it is difficult to bluff, the former because
the actual language employed is almost incompre-
hensible, and the latter because it is based largely on
the names of horses' parents. Either one knows these
or one does not. There is no middle way.

CHAPTER XV

THE SICK ROOM

Although it might be desirable for the sick to be segregated from the well, or as goes the old French adage, "*Chacun à son toux*", it is usual for those indulging in the common cold to continue their *modus vivendi* until the crisis is past. Having blown their way through the days and nights and through everyone's pocket handkerchiefs, and having defied all efforts to get them to bed, it is customary, the moment anxious attention is diverted from their misfortune, for them to collapse like balloons and assume the horizontal.

The first thing to remember about a patient in bed is that he is mentally deficient. He is also deaf, inaudible and nearly invisible. This enables you to discuss his symptoms across his prostrate body with relatives or visiting firemen without having to resort to him at all for information; indeed any information he cares to give must be regarded as puerile. If he says, "I really feel miles better", you should turn to his sister and say, "He still has a temperature, you know, and is not at *all* well!". If he says, "I would like to get up now", you must say (to his sister, of course), "We hope to have him up by next Wednesday". It is a good thing to arrange beforehand the exact day on which a patient may be allowed to feel better and to see that on no account does he register any improvement previous to it. Medical laws must be obeyed with scrupulous rigidity regardless of the patient's views on his condition, for in renouncing health he must also renounce the power to think, feel, speak, know, hear, or to wish for anything better than tapioca pudding.

If a patient insists on being spoken to, then he must be addressed in the third person as though he were a baby. "Does he want his little book on Ethnology then? He *shall* have his little book on Ethnology, but he must just wait till we've given him the doctor's lully medicine, m'm? Poor darling. Poor ickle sick thing. There, there . . . m'm?" and then he must be pulled forwards by the front of his pyjamas to have his pillows plumped out, have his face washed with a damp sponge because he is still too young to wash it himself, shoved back with a firm maternal hand and tucked up so tightly he can't breathe. It is useless for him to speak. Nurses, whether amateur or professional, are merely exaggerated nannies and lapse happily into that chronic state of deafness which is the nanny's chief bulwark against insanity. A patient's querulous queries, as a child's, can easily be answered while the mind is otherwise employed. A soothing timbre to the voice is all that is required.

For the patient himself there are certain rules to which he should strictly adhere. It is a good thing to keep relatives on the run, as this distracts their minds and prevents them from brooding; so the moment they have brought you the papers ask them if they'd be angels and pop downstairs and get a book you left on the hall table? This procured, ask them if they'd be saints and pop downstairs and get some writing paper? Alas, no pencil! Would they be absolutely dears and pop down and get one? And now the wireless? That's marvellous, but could they bear to pop down just once more and get the "Radio Times"? Oh dear, and now the point of the pencil has bust! Would it be possible ...? And a jug of water? Well, of course, if it *could* have some ice in it ... oh, and the telephone books?

Male patients should be rather "difficult" and however ill they are feeling should evince a wilful desire to "arise and go now". They should try, however sick it makes them, to smoke pipes, and it does not come

I

amiss to have a bottle of port concealed where it can most easily be found by a ministering angel. These *enfantillages* have a very stimulating effect on the maternal instincts in a woman, who likes her man to show a boyish and adventurous spirit in spite of his sufferings.

Female patients, on the other hand, should show a marked disinclination to get up and when visited by gentlemen should endeavour to look as though they would be in bed for such ages they would have to get another bedjacket trimmed with marabout from *somewhere*. They should look frail but not ugly, delicate but pinkly so. In fact, ladies cannot afford to be really ill. They should aim wholeheartedly for indisposition.

While on the subject of bed it is well to consider meals partaken therein. Even when trays with four little legs are provided the distance between the plate and the mouth is enormous. A napkin tied round the neck is always advisable, for there is nothing so discouraging to the well-wisher as to visit an invalid sprinkled with pieces of boiled cod. Besides, a bib completes the picture of helpless infancy so desirable in the sick.

Never eat toast in bed. Toast is intensely susceptible to the force of earthly gravitation and it finds its level beneath the lower portions of the body without fail. The irritation set up by one modest crumb is enough to raise a temperature to fever pitch.

On visiting the sick there is one point which super-
sedes all others for importance and should be remembered even at the risk of breaking a blood vessel. This
is to refrain from eating the muscat grapes you have
brought with you. It is all too easy in the course of conversation to eat right through the bunch, leaving but a
few green blobs on the ends of sticks when you go, but
you have no idea how this odious behaviour reacts on
an invalid's nervous system. He cannot very well
shout "Stop!", but in his weak condition the additional burden of this callous piece of requisitioning
may well send the tears gushing from his eyes to
course in salty rivulets down his ravaged countenance.
So hold back. Desist. Be resolute.

Do not sit on a patient's bed. However wide it may
seem there is never a sufficiency of room for his legs as
well as your posterior. The weight of the latter cants
the mattress to an uncomfortable angle as well as so
tightly binding the former with the bedclothes that
circulation comes to a halt and there is a very real danger of gangrene setting in.

There is no more tiring activity than talking to
someone in bed. Talking from a bed is, it is true,
equally tiring, but at least one is lying down. Conversation should never be allowed to flag for an instant,
but in however many directions it flows it should be
deflected from coursing towards despondent subjects,

such as death or the operations from which your
friends have failed to recover. A patient must, of
course, be allowed to describe his symptoms but it
is unkind to remind him that your cousin Edith had
just the same sort of thing two years ago and she is
still flat on her back with a lot of tubes inside her. It is
also churlish to tell amusing stories with regard to the
forceps, scissors and other medical tools which are so
frequently discarded by the medical profession in
people's tummies. Gossip is all right provided it is im-
personal. Cut off from the world save through the
media of wireless, papers, telephone, letters, books,
television and bush telegraph, a patient likes to hear of
the trials being undergone by those in the swim, especially as he can in no wise be expected to assist in any
way. However it is definitely fourth-rate to attempt
amusing a patient by suggesting that his wife is having
an affair during his enforced *accouchement*, and startling bits of news such as the imprisonment of his
grandmother for fraud or the elopement of his daughter with a duke should be left for others to divulge.

A short, high-pressured visit is preferable to a long,
low-pressured one, but any sort of visit is equivalent
for fatigue to swimming the Channel backwards in a
gale.

CHAPTER XVI

SERVANTS

A SUBTLE MEANS of ingratiating one-self with one's friends is to pay marked attention to their servants (if any). On all festive occasions, such as Christmas, Easter, St Valentine's Day and New Year's Day, not to mention the 4th of June, the 14th of July, Derby Day, Armistice Day, All Hallowe'en and one's own birthday, it is etiquette to proffer them large presents, and on all ordinary days of the week it is correct to ring them up and ask how they are and tell them how much their cooking, dusting and other feats of arms are appreciated. These small attentions, costly as they may be, are designed to form little ten-drils in the servile heart which will eventually find themselves clinging so tenaciously to the main stem and its friendly branches that no power on earth can prise them off. Many a maid has stayed with a man for no other reason than that she could not bear to be without his friend Colonel Prout's weekly visit to her kitchen bearing messages of admiration and bottles of old and tawny.

That well established catch-phrase *Pas devant les domestiques*!" is now obsolete, seeing that any *domestique* anybody is likely to have is bound to understand every language *except* English. Most households these days are run with the aid of a dictionary, and it is really extraordinary how many women know what a fishcake is in Polish.

It might be supposed that charladies, rising as they do when the cocks of Cricklewood crow their first adieu to the retreating stars, speeding as they do from Bow to Belgravia while the lamps are still lit, paddling as they do from Peckham on cold wet winter mornings ... well, anyhow, it might be imagined that charladies leave their inordinately distant homes to come to your aid in order to bolster their finances. But this is not so. They come to talk. If, by some chance so extraordinary it smacks of blood relationship with the Minister of Labour, you have in your possession another hand-maid, you need pay scant attention, but should your charlady form the whole of your staff it is not only etiquette but essential for you to be present during the

whole of her visit. Every charlady has a huge number
of relatives and acquaintances whose lives are fraught
with mystery, romance, adventure and, above all, co-
incidence. Unless you wish to be abandoned it is
absolutely vital for you to listen to a play-by-play com-
mentary on the astounding things that happen to
them. Riposte on your part is neither necessary nor desirable. Beyond an occasional "um?" or "really?" you
need not go, for all a charlady needs, in common with
Mark Antony, is to be lent ears. Never attempt to
trace your way through the maze of humanity which
will be placed before you. Never seek exactitude or
clarification or try to disentangle Gert from Daisy.
When faced with some such phrase as "Bert's Ethel
had ever such a shock last night! She thought she saw
Gracie coming down the stairs, and, d'you know, it
was Gracie come in the back way!" pretend to the
omniscience with which you are credited, and never,
never ask why or who. Interruptions only destroy the
narrative and tend to irritate.

After months of listening to this sort of thing you
may or may not be confident that it is Gert who has
such an overpowering horror of shellfish, and that Ed
(ex-R.A.F. with the bad knee) is the one who is married to Connie who cleans at the Odeon; but if you are
not absolutely positive do not fret. "Good Lord!",
"Well, well!" and, best of all, "Oh!" will get you by

and will effectively conceal your abysmal ignorance. Even when it is stated that your new dress sounds to Beryl as though it would not be at all to her fancy, do not succumb to pique and say, rather sharply, "And who the hell is Beryl?" because by this time you really should know.

In order to retain the services of your employee as well as a measure of sanity, it is well to assume the appearance of some receptacle, and although it may be a little difficult to look like a mother confessor it is perfectly easy to look like a bottomless well.

For those phenomenal ladies who can boast, even if only temporarily, of two or more servants, it is necessary to devote a portion of every day to the oozing of charm. This is very fatiguing, but it must be done and, what is more, it must be done equilaterally. No one department should be charmed beyond another. Owing to the rigid etiquette practised below stairs and the strong atmosphere of the closed shop which permeates the kitchen and pantry, it is inadvisable to the point of suicide to send a message from one to the other. Render unto Gladys the things which are Gladys's and never, by any chance, transmit them through Mabel. Thus if a friend is coming to stay with you the information should be given personally to each individual servant in your home, and garnished with appropriate noises of distress and cries of encouragement.

It is also a bad plan to discuss one servant with another, for the result is invariably distressing and the discovery invariably made that nobody can abide anybody else at any price whatever. There was once a lady who, in a misguided moment, asked her cook if she had heard the housemaid say anything about leaving. "I can't say as I 'ave, madam", she replied, "but then we 'aven't spoke for three years."

Until the volcano erupts it is more comfortable to close the ears to its rumblings and to have a notice placed on the far side of the green baize door marked "Do Not Disturb".

CHAPTER XVII

TIPPING

THERE ARE a number of people in this world who consider tipping to be a degrading thing, but though they may spend their whole lives considering it, from every angle and in every light, they cannot but conclude, if they are at all observant, that those at the receiving end of this undemocratic gesture *like* being degraded and get rather cross when they are not.

That there is an art in tipping cannot be denied. Gone are the days when a lady simply said, "Here, my man", and dropped a sixpence from lavender-gloved fingers into the hand of some cringing member of the lower orders, for, as everybody knows, there are no lower orders nowadays. Indeed one of the many confusing things about socialism is that though one has to

remember that everybody is equal it is still expected of
the rich to distribute largesse to the poor in appreciation of services already paid for in national taxes.
Habits, however, die hard, and a lady may find that in
the same way as she automatically supports hospitals
she is already supporting through the National Health
Insurance Scheme, so is it expected of her to supple-
ment the wages of those employed by her own British
Railways. Whatever she may feel about the matter,
there so rarely seems to be a moment, stations being
what they are, when she can get together quietly with
a porter to enquire of him whether he does not think it
a bit *infra dig* to accept tips from joint shareholders,
and it seems simplest to carry on as before or, if she
holds strong views, to carry her own bag.

To return to the mechanics of the thing, it is fairly
simple to tip porters, taxi drivers and chambermaids,
for the size of the tip is more or less fixed by the size of
the suitcase, the length of the taxi ride and the grand-
eur of the hotel. Waiters, too, need not be a worry to
the inexperienced, as 10 per cent of the bill plus a small
benefice is the usual thankoffering, accompanied of
course by a ravishing smile; but in the realms of the
unexpected the art of tipping really comes into its own,
for balanced against those who like being tipped quite
enormously there are those to whom the proffer of a
warm half-crown is a grave offence, and who shy away

from it like insulted horses. To offer a tip and have it refused is an unpleasant experience, and indeed any man with an ounce of grace in him will accept a tip immediately, be he an unidentified millionaire or an unrecognisable duke. In all the best drawing-room comedies dukes are mistaken for their butlers or gardeners, and they invariably accept remunerations from their future sons-in-law with an endearing courtesy. In real life this does not, perhaps, happen so often, but in these days it would be a very silly duke who did not snatch at every florin he could lay hands on. There are those men, however, lacking in grace but rich in pride, who rebuke the would-be tipper with disdainful gestures and an I'm-as-good-as-you-are look in the eye, and these reprimands are so painful to receive it is advisable to avoid them at all costs. Employ subterfuge. Let the insult, if it is to be an insult, get lost in a veil of words, a veil liberally perforated with loop-holes as well as being of a woolly texture.

Take, for instance, that nice young man on a motor cycle who stops and mends your puncture. That he is unbelievably precious and dear to you goes without question, but what else is he? Is he a chartered accountant with strangely dirty hands or a mechanic with strangely clean ones? And whichever he is, how does it help? Are all mechanics venal and all accountants proud? Is not the white collar as worthy of hire as the overall? And anyway, his collar isn't white, it's mauve, and he is wearing a smart blue suit . . . yet he hasn't a tie . . . yet he *has* a silk paisley handkerchief . . . yet . . . Doubtless you gaze in anguish at the nape of his neck as he struggles in the dust at your feet, praying that it may in some mysterious way give you guidance. It does not, of course, for necks are rarely voluble. Even accents, these days, are not indicative of a man's character. The only thing to do, as is so often the case in moments of stress, is to be frightfully brave. Holding a 10/– note firmly in one hand approach the creature boldly, and, giving him a smile of indescribable beauty, say "Thank you very, very much and as I have taken up so much of your time I should be so happy if you would buy your wife a little something with this". The logic contained in this remark is not, perhaps, obtrusive, but if spoken rather quickly and earnestly it sounds exactly as though it meant something. The alternatives, depending largely on womanly intuition, are "to send to your favourite charity", "to put on the winner of the 2.30" or "to buy one for the road as I'm sure you're dreadfully thirsty after saving my life!" You can also say, of course, "How much do I owe you for the use of your lovely spanner!" but this sometimes sounds a little forced, especially if he has been using yours. The main thing is to make a tip look like a present, and the giving of it a gesture of spontaneous gratitude rather than an act of condescen-

sion. Only practice makes perfect, but a lady need not
fear she will lack for opportunities in which to polish
her style.

Another problem to be faced is the recompensing of
that tribe of gentlemen who, apparently stupefied by
your charm, have kept back bottles of whisky, procured last minute theatre tickets and surreptitiously
slipped you packets of Players. To press pound notes
into their hands, or even envelopes containing pound
notes, smacks unpleasantly of bribery, and yet, taking
the long view, looking with shaded eyes into the distant future, it is expedient that their corruption should
be rewarded. Gifts in kind rather than in coin are
somehow less obvious, and by a skilful interchange of
these gentlemen's wares the niceties of a not very nice
business can be profitably observed. Thus do you run
with the bottle of port so carefully handed you by Mr
Driver in a plain wrapping, to Mr McFadden, and, as
you give this to him with your compliments, you purchase one of his theatre ticket vouchers and run on
with it to Mr Sparks, who has, waiting for you, an
equally plain packet containing cigarettes, and with
these you return to Mr Driver. Although the day must
be marked down as one singularly lacking in material
gain, the invisible assets are enormous.

There remain those establishments where it is
earnestly requested of patrons that they should with-
hold any additional *douceurs* to the staff as 10 per cent

of the bill is placed in a pool on their behalf. It is customary not to pay the slightest attention to this; customary, but a pity.

There is also the small but thorny matter of Car
Park Attendants, whose services consist of sitting on
stones, looking like comatose walruses, at one end of a
Square while your car, successfully hidden from their
view by trees, sits at the other. That they have not the
smallest interest in your vehicle and no powers with
which to apprehend car thieves even if, which is highly improbable, they noticed them; that they do
nothing to assist you backing in and that you do not
need assistance anyway is of small importance. At the
sound of a slamming door these gentlemen gather up
their skirts, and trailing yards of woollen muffler behind them, come wuffling like the wind round the corner. So frail is human courage that, faced with their
unalterable determination to get sixpence for doing
nothing, it usually crumbles, it succumbs; but there
are yet, thank God, those who struggle to escape before it is too late. Climbing into their cars on all fours
they attempt, while still sitting on the floor, to drive
away unnoticed, and many an exciting chase has thus
taken place to the detriment of the traffic regulations,
not to mention Car Park Attendant's hearts, if they
have any. It may not be etiquette to deprive lazy old
men of their beer money, but it is tremendous fun.

CHAPTER XVIII

MUSIC

IN ATTENDING a concert it is well to re-member that however well acquainted with a piece of music you may be it is totally unnecessary to convey this familiarity to the rest of the audience. It is doubt-less a source of pride to you that the little twiddly bits at the end of the *adagio* are as known to you as your own name, but your neighbours would *much* rather you didn't sing them. In all public places the ego should be suppressed, and it should be taken as said that for once, nobody is interested in you. So do not play the piano on your knees or nod your head from side to side or tap with your feet, as this inevitably draws attention to yourself, an attention you can well afford to forego. The results of your musical education

K

can be exposed to the public during the interval when you have ample time to criticise the orchestra's interpretation of your favourite piece; how the *con brio* wasn't *brio* enough and how the contra-bassoon missed out two notes in the fourth bar of the *vivace*. This information will bring you immense prestige when given at the proper time, but its physical manifestations, so akin to a mild form of St Vitus's dance, will, during a performance, bring you nothing but opprobrium.

There are some composers—at the head of whom stands Beethoven—who not only do not know when to stop but appear to stop many times before they actually do. There is nothing brands a lady as unmusical so much as clapping enthusiastically in the middle of a piece, and it always is wisest to postpone applause until the conductor has not only laid down his baton but has turned *volte face* to the audience, when it may safely be presumed he is no longer conducting. Failing a conductor, when an artiste or artistes bows or bow, ladies can take this as a signal for vociferous hand-clapping or the beating of umbrellas on the ground or the crying of *bis*! *bis*! or any other more individualistic modes of appreciation, but until the performer has definitely disassociated himself from his instrument or, in the case of a *cantatrice*, from her handkerchief, it is hazardous to presume the end of an item has been reached. Many a Beethoven quartet has come to an obvious conclusion only to start up again after the *kleinest* of *pauses*, practically from the beginning.

It is also considered bad form to applaud the separate movements of an orchestral work, as this disturbs the atmosphere and wakes people up; but on the other hand it is good form to applaud the separate arias in *Madame Butterfly*. She and other overwrought heroines, such as La Tosca, La Traviata and Lammermoor, Lucia de, *love* singing everything twice and are disappointed when they are not asked to do so, but girls like Sieglinde and Brunnhilde really and truly have quite enough to do getting through their songs once, and should by no means be encouraged to repeat them.

Wagner's operas must always be listened to with a deep comatose reverence, and preparations, as for Confirmation or Communion, made prior to hearing them. The *motifs* should be picked out with one finger on the piano beforehand, the other fingers on the other hand being employed to pour sustaining beverages down the throat in anticipation of a long musical siege. The works of Wagner, like those of Beethoven, touch the fringes of eternity.

Ladies unconversant with operas would do well to choose as a beginning those of which the essence is

frequently distilled in tea-time music. There is nothing
so heartening for a lady than to know all the tunes,
even if these are considerably less compressed than in
the foyer of the Grand Hotel. *La Bohême* is a nice
opera to start with, but again let it be repeated, and in
this case even louder than before, familiarity with an
aria does not mean that a lady should join in. If she
gets carried away by the music let it be out of the opera
house.

It is perfectly easy to manage one's manners when
one goes to a concert in a public place, but "musical
evenings" in private houses are infinitely more difficult to cope with. The trouble is to know what to do
with one's face. There is really no more arduous task
given to man than to sit *facing* somebody while music
is being played, as however sternly the facial muscles
may be controlled, music has a way of appearing to release the soul from its prison and to plant it naked in
the eyes. An animated face hides many secrets, but one
that is in repose, and what is more is being dug at with
a violin, often reveals them with embarrassing accuracy. Then do the old look older, the unloved more
forlorn, the bereaved inconsolable; the young look
touchingly vulnerable and those who have made a
hash of their lives look, for the first time, as though
they were aware of the *ragout*. It is probable that all
these sad faces are veiling thoughts no more profound

than puddles; thoughts perhaps about egg pickling or
football pools, but because they are accompanied by
music they appear to onlookers to be dedicated solely
to unrequited love or the mutability of earthly joys.
Judging by the faces of others it is likely that one's
own face is registering some secret sorrow, and if it be
but grief that one has come to the party even this is
likely to be misconstrued. As, however, biology insists
on every person having a face there is little one can do
about it. The best way to avoid both one's own face
and the faces of others is to shut one's eyes. This sometimes sends one to sleep, but an alert hostess will
usually be sufficiently awake to note when an item on
the programme has drawn to a close, and her saying
"Enchanting!", or "Do play the little Ravel!", or
"Was that in D flat or C sharp?" will be enough to
arouse her guests from their stupor and bring their
hands together.

When two or more intimate friends are gathered in
one place for the purpose of listening to music it is
essential to hire musicians who are not in the least bit
funny. Perhaps the performer to be most guarded
against is the singer who gives literal translations of
foreign songs prior to singing them, *i.e.*, "This is a
little song about a Prince who went to woo a Princess
with a feather in his hat; and she says to him, 'Prince,
why do you wear a feather in your hat?' and he says,

'Princess, I do not know' ". On the whole singers are dangerous in merry company, as, even if they have not got funny faces to begin with, they eventually make them.

Harpists are rather dangerous too, as when they break the strings of their heavenly instruments, which happens frequently, they always go back to the beginning and start again with plucky determination, thereby frequently playing "Jardin sous la Pluie", or at any rate bits of it, three times before they bring it to a successful conclusion. If the audience is in the right mood for comedy, though the eyes be ever so hermetically sealed, waiting in a state of suspended animation for another string to break is apt also to break morale.

CHAPTER XIX

COCKTAIL
PARTIES

THERE ARE two ways of getting food for a cocktail party. One is to buy some bread, some potted shrimps, cheese and some sticks of celery and spend the whole afternoon trying to balance one upon the other. The second way is to order much the same things from a shop, the only difference being that the latter will be enshrouded in a film of gelatine, thereby being more flexible and more likely to go into the mouth than on to the carpet. Drink, of course, depends entirely on the state of the markets, both black and white, but it is always a good plan to give guests a potent brew to begin with, and only when this runs out to resort to less inflammable concoctions largely composed of lemonade. After a passage of time guests will not know what they are drinking, but at the start, when one very old uncle up from the country and one very shy undergraduate down from Oxford are the only guests confronting each other across the large expanse of strangely dirty carpet, gin is the thing. Gin is the greatest evil of our time, but on its way to rot the stomach it titillates the tongue and sets it wagging.

It is sensible to mix the cocktails in adequate quantities before the guests arrive, as a hostess who is never to be found except drawing corks in the kitchen is not fulfilling her duties. When things have got properly going, of course, she will not be missed, and her guests will not have the smallest desire to see her and no intention at all of saying good-bye and thanks awfully, but at the beginning, before they have found their own way to the drinks, she should be on the *tapis* to press them into their hands.

Naturally enough a hostess on the brink of a cocktail party wants her room to look as nice as possible, and she will therefore spend most of the day planting ashtrays on the tables, both occasional and otherwise, only to transplant them later on. She will move the shrimps from the piano to the pouffe and the flowers from near the fire to near the fauteuil; she will push chairs back and pull chairs in and count the glasses innumerable times and smooth the rugs and straighten the pictures and then move the shrimps back to the piano. Although she may spend many hours thus employed and will be under the impression the room is as elegant as she can make it, five minutes after the first guest has arrived she will perceive that in the very centre of the mantelpiece there rests a thermometer, a bottle of ink, two orange sticks and an india rubber. All cocktail hostesses are conversant with variants of this phenomenon, of which there is, to date, no explanation. Some find the can from which they have filled the flower vases sitting in the middle of the Bristol glass; others find secateurs nestling against the olives, and some have even been known to discover tubes of toothpaste lurking behind the bridge rolls, this latter being a supernatural manifestation of such extraordinary complexity as to defy human comprehension. Because of the prevalence of this occupational malady among cocktail hostesses it is wise for them to invite someone outside the family circle to come early to review the situation. A fresh eye will do wonders, and though it may demand that the shrimps be moved yet again and that all the furniture be taken back to the place from whence it came, it will also be swift to mark the knitting bag in the coal scuttle and the kitchen knife amid the snuff boxes.

It is etiquette for a hostess to have a terrible stomach ache at three minutes past six and to k n o w that no one is coming.

It is not done to let anybody be too happy. The moment two people are seen to be enjoying one another's company, a good hostess introduces a third element or removes the first. There should always be an atmosphere of quest, those at the door seeking to get in, those by the piano seeking to reach the fire, and many lost souls seeking to reach each other. At a really successful party their every effort is thwarted, thus causing their struggles to become more pronounced and their voices more hysterical. A drawing-room should, in fact, be turned into a tiny hell, just about as hot and just about as confused.

Incidentally, in introducing the famous to the infamous neither too little nor too much should be said. "And this, my dear, is THE Christopher Slack" is by itself insufficient recommendation to one who has never heard of the poor man, and may lead the alarmed guest to make desperate but erroneous assumptions as to Mr Slack's function in life. On the other hand, to say: "This is Christopher Slack who, as you *know*, is a famous economist and has just written a book, which I am *sure* you have read, called 'What, no Sterling?'" implies it is highly improbable that *anybody* has heard of him. Although a hostess, like Martha, is cumbered about with much serving, she does well to find time in which to notify one guest of an impending introduction to another, and to give a brief outline of his case

history. Thus can guests approach each other with
confidence, as well primed with facts as they are with
stuffed olives.

At the end of a cocktail party there are always two
or three people who will not or cannot go. Embedded
in a sofa like roots of oak trees in the earth they remain,
smiling benevolently out on to the scene of devastation
and saying "*Lovely* party, darling. The *greatest* fun".
It is not always easy to gain access to the minds of these
fuddled derelicts, but if such remarks as "Do have
another drink before you GO?" or "Now the party's
OVER and NOBODY else is coming, do finish off the
radishes!" have no effect, a hostess may strive to speed
the undeparting guests by taking off her shoes and
ostentatiously emptying the ashtrays, collecting the
glasses, and carrying them all away into the kitchen.
If this somewhat drastic procedure is unavailing it can
safely be assumed that what is sitting on the sofa is
stewed. Pickled guests should either be left where
they are or, if they are conscious, should be led gently
down the stairs and put into a hastily summoned
vehicle. From no lady's cocktail party should a guest
ever be *carried*. Any lady who has friends liable to be
called for by ambulances is no lady. She is just a
woman who shouldn't give cocktail parties.

A lady who only knows her husband at a cocktail
party need not be too depressed, for although it may

seem rather a waste of time to dress up in a drinking costume in order to stand in a crowd and talk to him, many husbands and wives have had extraordinarily interesting conversations in such circumstances. Forced by the rules of etiquette to appear animated and even happy, they have abandoned their usual topics of talk, consisting as they so frequently do of queries regarding temporal matters which can be answered monosyllabically or merely by optic implication, and have plunged into subjects on which since their engagements they have had no time or desire to ponder; subjects such as God, Existentialism, Stamp Collecting and so forth. Sometimes this proves such a novel experience and they become so amazed at themselves they separate with the greatest reluctance. It is a tragedy that marriage has such a stultifying effect on verbal intercourse, so much so that one forgets the beloved has views which he is able to express clearly and at some length on matters far removed from racing, the whereabouts of his pipe or the idiosyncrasies of the plumbing system, and the one good thing about a cocktail party . . . there are few other good things . . . is that it sometimes forces these views out into the open. Nevertheless a hostess feels somewhat uneasy at the sight of a married couple talking and laughing with each other. There is something vaguely improper about it.

CHAPTER XX

CORRESPONDENCE

STATIONERY used by a lady is remarkable for nothing so much as its simplicity. The colour is either white, cream, grey or what is known as azure. It is never puce or pink. The lettering bears no flourishes or curlicues. The edges of the paper are not bevelled, neither are they bordered in bright colours. A peeress is permitted to place on the flaps of her envelopes a small coronet, so that the recipients of her letters may, before reaching the subject matter, feel that quick thrill of joy which all contact with the aristocracy must inevitably bring to those less favoured; but anything save a coronet, *i.e.*, a crest or a monogram, is not lady-like. s.w.a.k. or xxx may be employed, of course, by anybody, but these should be written in longhand, and *never* embossed.

L

Ink should be blue—invariably, unswervingly, un-flinchingly. Even the tiniest note written in the palest green ink hurtles a lady down into the demi-monde with a reverberating crash, and it may take gallons of Stephens' blue-black or Waterman's black-blue to get her afloat again.

LETTERS OF THANKS. To write a bread and butter letter too soon after returning from a visit appears as though you were anxious to get the whole thing cleared up as quickly as possible and get down to the business of living normally again, whereas a hostess prefers to think you are mulling over the joys experienced at her expense and relishing them like old brandy. Twenty-four hours should be allowed to elapse before you put pen to paper. On the other hand, to wait a week before you write denotes nothing so much as forgetfulness, and you must perforce begin your rapture by apologising for the delay *in detail*. "I have been frightfully busy lately", is not quite good enough. It is more polite to qualify, *i.e.*, "My maid has got jaundice", or "I have strained my femur playing rummy", or "I found I *was* expected to act Desdemona after all".

Letters can be brief but should never stray one millimetre from the point. Graphic descriptions of train journeys, skids in taxis or the condition of the home on reaching it are of small value to a hostess thirsting for appreciation. Truth need not be betrayed, for once, and ambiguous phrases such as "I have never *known* such food!" or "*What* a house!" can be penned with an easy conscience seeing that they will undoubtedly be received in a trustful spirit. In one of the classics there is a letter which reads:

"Thank you a thousand times. Thanks, and again thanks.

Yours etc.

P.S. Many thanks."

but although this is a perfect letter in its way and can in no wise be misconstrued, it lacks that little extra something so dear to the heart of a hostess; the tender regard for her tulips, the loving respect for her mayonnaise, the joy of meeting her grandmother. It is the little things, my friends, that count in the end; which may remind you that you have returned home with only three knitting needles. A request for the fourth to be despatched by passenger train should be added in a postscriptum or, as it is sometimes called, a P.S. (See above.)

LETTERS OF CONDOLENCE. Letters of condolence should be written not so much with an eye to the bereaved as with a recollection of the departed. The bereaved *know* they are going to feel miserable and lonely, and repeatedly to point this out to them and thus draw a large circle of words round the vacuum in their lives is not comforting. Rather should you stress the qualities they held most dear in the departed and rejoice in the remembrance of them. If you do not know exactly what these were the christianly virtues are always at your disposal.

BUSINESS LETTERS. Drones do not often write business letters, but when they do they should do their utmost to squeeze in the words *inst.* and *ult.* "Dear Mr Coleport, thank you for yesterday's letter . . ." is a horribly amateurish beginning, whereas, "Dear Sir, your letter of the 15th inst. just come to hand . . ." shows that you are not to be trifled with and probably own a filing cabinet. It is hard, admittedly, to sustain this note for the whole length of a letter, but the smallest lapse is fatal. The tiniest deviation from pomposity dooms you to eternal patronisation. If in a moment of feminine weakness you write, "I don't understand one bit what you mean in that bit about the money Aunt Aggie left me!" you are proved ripe for condescension, but for some reason, if you write, "I fail to comprehend the import of your remarks re the reversionary interest that has now matured as the result of my late father's late sister's demise", although this does nothing to lighten the darkness, and indeed adds somewhat to the confusion, you are immediately treated seriously as one who will brook no nonsense and will take the whole thing up to the House of Lords if needs be.

It is all a question of pride and the price you are willing to pay for it. Etiquette may demand that business letters should be couched in a language as remote from everyday usage as possible, but you may find that after many months of decoding such missives (usually it costs 6/8 a time to do this), and coding replies, there will come a moment when you get tired of it all and thirst to drink at the sweet waters of knowledge. In fact, quite simply, you would like someone to tell you in words of one, or at the most two, syllables whether Aunt Aggie has left you £100, £1,000 or merely some useless shares in a Peruvian Ice Cream factory. This is when stamina tells. Some people throw in the sponge with a shamelessly abandoned gesture and confess all, writing, in longhand:

"Dearest Mr Coleport, you are the sweetest old thing in the world, but I simply haven't the foggiest idea what any of your letters have meant *ever* and as I want to buy a fur coat perhaps you'd be an absolute angel and tell me how much of Aunt Aggie's legacy I can lay my hands on *now*."

Others, feeble but still fighting, hope to adhere to the proprieties and yet gain information by typing:

"Dear Sir,

As I find myself in somewhat straitened circumstances and have various obligations I do not wish to forego and a number of commitments I feel impelled to meet, I would be obliged if you could inform me as to the extent of the amount of the hereunto beforementioned avuncular legacy that can be realised in cash sterling, to be utilised in discharging debts accrued during the interim period between the demise of the person concerned and the granting of probate.

I remain,

Yours truly,

Ethel Spriggs

(Mrs Herbert Spriggs)

R. G. Coleport Esq.,
962, Victoria Street,
London, S.W.1.,
England."

The point of typing the name and address of the gentleman with whom you are communicating on the bottom left-hand corner of the letter is not so much to remind him of them as to suggest that you are keeping a carbon copy of the correspondence.

LOVE LETTERS. It is etiquette to write love letters
in pencil on odd scraps of paper torn from jot pads,
and to be really thorough they should be written at
night and torn up in the morning.

Although lovers pay particular attention to post-
men and know to the exact minute when they will
reach their doorsteps, they are rather slack about
memorising the times of local postal *collections* and the
resultant times of delivery, which in very truth they
would do well to note; for love letters at breakfast are
somewhat indigestible. If you are a man it is not easy
to believe that your "mouth is a madness", when you
are cramming the last piece of toast into it before
tearing off to catch the tube, and if you are a woman
the morning is so punctuated by various misfortunes,
by broken hoovers, leaking taps, fused wires, burnt
holes, mildewed cheese, laddered stockings, torn
sheets, men to read the meter and feckless friends on
the telephone, it is impossible not to think the beloved
was drunk when he wrote "You are always so calm
and quiet, my darling, as cool as the long grass at even-
tide, as fresh as the dew on a rose, as soothing and
peaceful as a lullaby". Round about tea-time you can
believe this sort of thing, for as the day progresses so
do the more utilitarian aspects of life retreat, and
magic, no longer interrupted by news of mislaid cauli-
flowers and burst hot-water bottles, steals from its

hiding place to cover you in a haze of wishful thinking.

LETTERS OF INTRODUCTION. When writing a
letter of introduction the one important thing to remember is that as etiquette demands it should be
placed in an unsealed envelope, the bearer will without
a shadow of doubt read it. It should therefore be im-
personal and signify practically nothing save that the
hand which carries it is attached to a body on which
your personal eyes have rested.

"Dear Joanna,
    This is to introduce to you my good friend, Eva
Battersthwaite, who is passing through Johannes-
burg on her way to Dar es Salaam. She is a splendid
person, has been working with me on the A.D.C.
for years, and any kindness you can show her I shall
consider as a kindness to me.
    She brings you my love.

                                    Yours ever,
                                        Adela".

That is all that is required. It merely gives Eva an
entrée into Joanna's life. In another letter, despatched
hot airmail, you can be considerably more expansive
and warn Joanna that she will most certainly dislike
Eva very much indeed as she has no sense of humour
and talks about "dossing down on the couch", but will

Joanna please, out of the goodness of her heart, give Eva a cup of tea and perhaps introduce her to a Bishop or something equally holy? She really has a heart of gold, has Eva, which is a terrible thing to have, but she has also got three pairs of pince-nez suspended on different coloured elastics from her bosom, which are quite amusing sometimes. Anyway, even if Joanna curses you like a trooper, will she just see the old thing for a few minutes?

This letter must on no account, not even inadvertently, be placed in the same envelope as the letter of introduction.

CHAPTER XXI

AT THE
HAIRDRESSER'S

PSYCHOLOGISTS should have a lot to
say about hairdressers. There they are, small dark men
with combs in their hands; nothing out of the ordinary
to look at, tending to be French but otherwise designed on orthodox lines. Yet to most ladies they are as
priests. On entering a hairdressing cubicle a lady to all
intents and purposes enters a confessional box, and
there is nothing on earth, no secret however sacred, no
scandal however intimate she will not divulge to her
beloved Monsieur Henri. It has never been discovered why having the hair washed should release a
lady's innermost thoughts unless it be that a brisk
stimulation of the scalp incites her inhibitions to break
loose from their normal bonds; nor is it known why

she should so mislay her powers of perception as to believe that the cubicle she is in is soundproof. Even if the partitions do not reach the ceiling she is not deterred. Like an ostrich with its head in the sand is a lady with her head in the drier.

The following conversation is typical and should be copied by all ladies who wish to be in the height of fashion.

"Oh, Monsieur Henri, Monsieur Henri, I'm most frightfully pleased to see you T H E most frightful thing has happened! My husband has left me!"

"Oh, Madame! Pas possible? Excuse me please . . . Lydia, the scissors!"

"He's gone off with some awful blonde from a flower shop! Oh God, isn't life ghastly . . . I only want it thinned this week, Henri, not shortened."

"Bien, Madame. He will come back of course. These little escapades, you know . . . I am leaving the sides . . ."

"But I don't want him back! This is the second time it's happened and if he thinks he can go on kicking me around he's mistaken . . . I thought you might give me a brightening shampoo to-day?"

"Certainly, Madame".

"God, I need brightening! But look, Henri, this is a deathly secret, you know? I don't want the whole world to know he's done it *again*. It's too humiliating.

Not that I haven't done it to him too! I'm a damned sight more attractive than he thinks! Wow! That's most terribly hot!"

"Ah, pardon! Lydia, it is too hot for Madame. Voyons, Madame, you must not fret. Love has so many tricks up her sleeves and the poor human heart . . ."

"WHAT?"

"Nothing, Madame. There, all clean and fresh. You wish it high, *à la Marquise?*"

"I wish I were dead!"

"Mais non, Madame, non!"

"I shall ring up Teddy Fitzgerald and make him take me out. We had an affair you know, a long time ago."

"Yes, I remember . . . the brilliantine, Lydia."

"He was sweet. He kissed divinely. Oh, Henri, you are such a comfort, but please, please don't forget it's frightfully secret . . . oh, this infernal drier!"

"Je vous jure . . ."

"WHAT?"

"Je repète JE VOUS JURE THAT NO ONE SHALL KNOW YOUR HUSBAND HAS LEFT YOU!"

"OH, THANKS."

"Pas de quoi".

"OH, HENRI, COULD I HAVE 'THE TATLER' PLEASE?"

"Miss Lydia, *The Tatler* for Madame St George".

CHAPTER XXII

COMMITTEES

ONE OF THE foremost duties of a lady is to sit on Committees. A Committee is merely a gathering of people who, unable to agree individually on a given subject, are determined to reach collective unanimity even if it takes all summer, which it very often does. The given subject is invariably of a philanthropic nature, for the idea that ladies are rich and lead leisurely lives dies hard, and moreover it is unladylike not to appear interested in the welfare of others.

Committee meetings are always held at inconvenient times and usually take place in dark, dusty rooms the temperatures of which are unsuited to the human body. Sometimes they take place in somebody's dining-room, and this is to be encouraged, for although the faint smell of yesterday's brussels sprouts is not conducive to concentrated thought, the very fact that sooner or later someone will want to come and lay the table acts as a goad to the proceedings, a spur to the dozing brain cells.

All Committees have Chairmen and these must be addressed in the masculine or neuter gender, *i.e.*, Mr or Madam Chairman. "Madam Chairwoman", though logical, is wrong, and so of course is, "Oh, Muriel dear, *no*!" Ceremony must be stood on with firmness even when the Committee members are on the friendliest terms, and the use of christian names must be rigorously barred. A Chairman, even though she be surrounded by her kith and kin, should not say, "Dearest ones, shall I sign these thingummybobs now?" but rather, "Is it your pleasure I should sign these minutes?" and then both the kith and the kin signify the affirmative by raising the right hand. Incidentally, nobody has ever been known to say, "No, it isn't".

A Good Chairman will have a booming voice, a commanding eye and an aptitude for beating a tattoo with a gold pencil. A very good Chairman never lets anybody speak at all but assumes with perfect confidence and with a perfect disregard for the truth that everybody is in agreement. The very best Chairman of all allows the Committee's secretary who, as she is paid, is the only person in the room who knows what she is there for, to take charge of the Meeting, to make pronouncements, to read letters demanding replies which she has already drafted and to request for decisions which she has already taken.

A lady should endeavour to keep awake as long as possible, but there is no cause for panic should she be rudely awakened by an enquiry as to what she, Miss White-Wilkinson, thinks. The simple phrase "I agree with the last speaker" is quite sufficient to quell suspicion in the minds of her colleagues. If she can see her way to passing a note from time to time saying "Surely this should be dealt with by the Finance Committee?", or "I'm sure the Board of Trade would never allow it" or, of course, "Can you lunch on Friday?" she can drop off between whiles without a qualm.

It sometimes becomes apparent during a Committee meeting that in the not distant future *action* of one kind or another may have to be taken. To swell the funds, gain adherents or spread the tidings it may be decided that a house to house canvass should be put in train, that tickets for a ball or a film *première* must be sold or, most likely, that the 20,000 envelopes addressed last Saturday should be re-opened, re-stuffed and re-addressed by next Saturday. Common decency forbids a lady to refuse outright to trudge, hawk or lick just simply because she doesn't want to. Bad

M

health has to be very bad indeed if it is to be more of a handicap to a lady than it is to her equally inventive colleagues. Only one thing can save her. A regretful admission that during all the relevant hours in which the needed work can be done she will be sitting on other Committees. These need have no relation to or connection with the one she is at present attending, for in the eyes of Committee members all Committees are sacred. Murmuring something about the Women's League on Tuesday, the Housing Sub-Committee on Wednesday and the Holiday Fund on Thursday a lady can continue to live in elegance and indolence, scrubbing the floors and queuing for cod, while preserving the appearance, so necessary to her self-respect, of a *Grande Dame*.

CHAPTER XXIII

MOTORING

FOR A DRIVER to be driven by somebody else is always an ordeal, for there are only three types of drivers: the too fast, the timid and oneself. No greater call is made upon the fortitude of a man than to ride with a fast but loose driver unless it be to ride with a slow tight one, although to ride with a fast tight one is worst of all, unless you happen to be with a slow loose one. Whatever your sufferings may be, however, the verbal expression of them must always be temperate and heavily disguised. Never proffer advice. However nervous you are never say, "I believe this is *quite* a bad crossing", or "The lights change *very* quickly here", or "You will be careful, dear, won't you, it's so skiddy to-day". Remarks such as these, casting, however obliquely, aspersions on the driver's capability, merely act as a challenge to his baser, exhibitionist side, and he will probably flaunt his fecklessness in a burst of outrageously bad driving. Again, though there may be just cause for you to scream and bury your face in your hands, the effect is always disastrous, as it takes the driver's mind off the plans, if any, he has for circumventing the approaching hazard.

Endurance and prayer are the primary require-ments for a passenger, or, failing these being readily to hand, wishful thinking and the faith of the ostrich. It makes things pleasanter, for instance, if you assume that the driver has control of his car, if you assume he has seen a rival vehicle emerging very fast from a side turning. If your powers of self-hypnosis are not equal to this, however, it is permitted to say, "By Jove, there's one of those new 14-cylinder Humming Birds! Going like stink too!" If he replies "What?" it may be too late to repeat the observation, in which case it will be possible to examine the cylinders at closer quarters: but if he says "Where?" there is just a chance he may raise his eyes from the speedometer which he has at last got over the 90 mark (been trying for years) and will give the matter his kind attention. This will make him cross, but will keep you alive, which is of such im-mense importance to so many people.

The occupational disease known as "curly-toes"

which is the bane of all nervous passengers can only be
healed by abandoning oneself to the belief of immor-
tality or by the contemplation of a past so pleasant (or
alternatively so odious) it no longer seems necessary to
prolong the human experience. Pushing with one's
feet against the floorboards does not help in the least.

There is another chronic car disease, less virulent
but still fairly infectious, which takes the form of a violent allergy on the part of the driver to stop and ask the
way. He will drive 50 miles off his route, stopping
every few miles to consult maps and signposts rather
than exchange a few civil words with a pedestrian. It is
true that pedestrians never know where they are—at
times one might suppose that England is filled with
lost souls pushing prams—but there is always a hope
that a postman or a policeman may have a suspicion as
to his whereabouts; but no, the mesmerised driver,
filled it would seem with a relentless pride, hurries on,
blindly seeking the narrow way that leads to Little
Blitherington, and finding it not. Of course there are
unexpected pitfalls in asking human beings for information, not the least being that it will be incorrectly
given. Once there was a man who asked a very old
gaffer if he could direct him to Cholmondeley-cum-
Salford, and the latter, so overexcited at being spoken
to for the first time for twenty years, swung his arm
round and said "It be yonder", this movement being

accomplished with such gusto that he fell over and broke his leg and had to be supported in hospital by the driver until he died.

The third car disease, which is an offshoot of the above, is the inability to find a suitable site for a picnic. This disease is so prevalent it is a serious breach of etiquette not to suffer from it. Woods full of bluebells, green banks by running streams, dingle dells and heather bells must be driven *past*, for the correct place in which to have a picnic is in a stone quarry on the main road *after* one has crossed Dartmoor.

Married driving calls for the utmost tact, for it is a strange thing in life that love breeds a singular lack of confidence, particularly in the male breast. No man worthy of the name considers his wife capable of understanding the simplest piece of mechanism and it is a recurring pain for him to have to sit impotently by while she mishandles his car. (The same does not apply to blondes who are even allowed to drive Bentleys for a little way, say from Slough to Maidenhead.)

Wives at the steering wheel would do well to play the innocent and in general give the appearance of novices without actually doing any of the frightful things novices do do. Enquiries as to why the car isn't pulling properly are always welcomed, but a husband should on no account be too eager to supply the answer. After a brief pause tokening puzzlement and interest he should say, "I wonder if by any chance the handbrake has got stuck again? You know how it does, darling!" The operative word here is *again*, without which the observation has a sarcastic tone, especially harmful to marital harmony. The strong smell of burning rubber need not be questioned nor silently underlined by the ostentatious lowering of a window.

Remarks such as, "Did you know you were still in second?" or "I should change down now if I were you" must be quashed before they reach the lips, as no marriage can survive them.

The doors of cars never shut properly for strangers, and it is etiquette for the owner to lean across his passenger's stomach and say "I'm so sorry, but it's a damnable door", and then slam it very hard on the passenger's coat.

Everyone over sixty thinks the window handle is the door handle. Everyone under ten thinks the horn should be permanently pressed down. Nobody over seventy can get into a car and nobody under six can get out of one, but both of them can *fall* out with insolent ease.

CHAPTER XXIV

FOREIGNERS

THE GREAT THING to remember about foreigners is that, without any exception, they are all quite certain they had a very much worse time in the war than the British. To point out that "we stood alone" has been in execrable taste for many years, as is all mention of bombs, black-outs and beastly experiences with stirrup pumps. War distress, whether past or present, has nothing whatever to do with England. It is FOREIGN.

To visitors from the American continent it is still etiquette to apologise for our lack of butter, coal, petrol, orange juice, soap, etc., and to add some abject comments on the scarcity of linen which precludes their having a clean face towel every day. On the other hand, to visitors from the once occupied countries it is etiquette to apologise for having any food, linen or fuel *at all*.

It is a good thing to know:

(*a*) The capitals of foreign countries.

(*b*) Roughly where they are on the map.

(*c*) Which side they were on in the war.

In the case of small islands such as the Andaman it is helpful to know whom they belong to and what is the normal colour of the inhabitants.

As regards what is left of the Empire, it is always wise to refresh one's memory with an atlas before embarking on any lengthy conversation with a British visitor from overseas, so to fix in one's mind which of the bits are Dominions, which Colonies, and which bits are neither Dominions nor Colonies but are known as The Commonwealth and The Union.

It is well to know the names of a few important people in each country over a certain size, the certainty of the size being computed from the number of people in it one knows the names of.

Canadians do not like to be told they speak with American accents, Australians with cockney or South Africans with Dutch.

It is better to remember that New Zealand is not a part of Australia—much better.

It is traditional etiquette not to like foreigners very

much but nevertheless to insist in the face of certain
evidence to the contrary that they are vastly superior
to us in all respects. It is not absolutely necessary to
say out loud that England is pathetic, gutless, lazy,
weak, vacillating and bankrupt, for this can be more
subtly inferred by delineating the strength, purpose,
integrity and richness of other lands. This deceives no
one, least of all the foreigner, who is often, it must be
regretfully stated, intelligent. All the same it is etiquette.

There is nothing against learning a few words of a
foreign tongue, but it is in extremely bad form to pronounce them properly.

Another useful thing to remember is that whatever
is disappointing or unpleasant in international affairs
is always the fault of the British, but in apologising for
this it is not necessary to assume that all foreigners are
deaf.

As English gentlemen are not versed in the art of
flattery, ladies may find themselves unequipped for
the blandishments offered them by foreigners, but it is
essential they should realise that alien compliments
are only equalled in charm by their insincerity. In the
last war, when England was invaded by America and
the latter's sons met the former's daughters for the
first time, the different shades of etiquette employed
for the strengthening of the *entente cordiale* led to a lot

of misunderstanding. Ladies who had been forced all
their lives to draw attention to themselves by pointing
and saying "*Look*! I've got a new hat!" found both
themselves and their sartorial embellishments being
spontaneously praised. This so went to their heads
they forgot that the seeming spontaniety was in fact a
purely mechanical gambit of conversation, a traditional corollary to "Hello, Beautiful!". Many a soft-
voiced southerner was astounded to find that a simple
little observation regarding his *vis à vis*' fictional
charms, tossed away as lightly as a word about the
weather, constituted a formal proposal of marriage.
"Gee", they sighed, to equally puzzled padres, "I
o n l y said I'd like to tie the whole world up in a bit of
blue ribbon and lay it at her feet! And now the girl
thinks I love her!" And they shook their round crew-
cut heads in wonder while the ladies, misty eyed with
dreams of Montana, collected coupons for a wedding
dress from their relatives. The clearing-up of these
misunderstandings was often painful, even when con-
ducted in the English language, but when, as was frequently the case, they had to be clarified in Polish, the
agony was exceptional.

It is very difficult for an English lady to remain
equipoised in the face of foreign adulation even if it is
not difficult for her to remain virtuous (which it often
is too). The sex is susceptible to all forms of cherishing,

and starved, as is the Anglican variety, of sweet nothings, of velvet looks and heavy sighs, it all too recklessly steps out on to the tightrope of *amour*, gets dizzy with inexperience, loses its balance and takes a header into the arms of the first French Count who has dropped in for tea and is merely expressing his thanks for the crumpets in the most civilised way he knows how.

Complete and instantaneous abandonment of all inhibitions is, of course, greatly to be deplored, but so is a rigid puritanism. It does not come amiss to have some idea of accepting a compliment gracefully. It is not, for instance, very friendly, when the Count says "You have ze skin of an angel, madame, un veritable peau d'ange; ze real English beauty, hein?" for you to answer "Oh rot!" or "Tell it to the Marines!" Between this and offering him your skin as a memento there lies a middle way. Simply thank him. Just say "Thank you," or "Thanks" or "Thanks awfully". This implies that you know all about your skin and he needn't bother to go on though you are quite grateful for his having mentioned it. The same method can be applied to compliments directed at your clothes. The answer to "Say, but that's a swell costoom, honey", is not "What, *this* old thing?" but again the simple words, "Thank you".

The trouble is, let us face it bravely, there is planted

in the English breast along with an exaggerated distaste for love an exaggerated regard for truth, and it is
faintly irritating to be told by a man that you have a
divine figure when Y O U know and H E knows and you
K N O W he knows it is nothing of the kind. It is all very
pleasant but pointless, and there is much to be said for
the Englishman's rare utterances, stammered though
they be through the stem of a pipe or spoken abruptly
as on the parade ground, for they have the value of being sincere and are usually based on fact, not fiction.

A tendency to assume that *everybody* in a foreign
country knows one another must be curbed, for as it is
very irritating to be asked by a Peruvian whether one
knows Miss Smith who lives in Shropshire, so is it
irritating for him to be asked whether he knows a Mr
McKay who is now living in his part of the world—
Chile or somewhere. The universe is small but it is not
as small as all that, and unless the subjects of these
questions are to be located in towns, and not very big
towns either, they are best left to live their own friend-
less lives.

In escorting foreigners round London it is etiquette
to pretend one has been to the Tower and to conceal
the fact that one has not set foot inside St Paul's since
the age of nine. On being asked what various buildings
are, answers should be given promptly and firmly,
even if incorrectly. Nobody can be quite certain which

is the Mansion House and which the Royal Exchange, but it couldn't matter less. There are an enormous number of enormous buildings in London which one has never noticed before, but it is in bad taste to be surprised to see them. A certain number of them are marked, and a quick, secret glance can decipher Moon Assurance Co. or Anglo-Ecuadorian Glassmakers' Association inscribed over the door, but a very large number are not, and it is up to the Cockney to prove her proverbial quick-wittedness. There are doubtless many names with which she is familiar and if she does not attach these to the right buildings it is of small moment, for the foreigner is unlikely to argue. Trinity House, Cannon Street Station, The Bank, the Odeon and Selfridge's are all suitable names to memorise, and when these run out a lady can always draw from the bottomless well of Masonic Halls. Although only a few of these are still standing she has but to invent some old-sounding tradesmen, *i.e.*, Plate-layers, Salt-sifters, Hoopers, Tankermen and the like, and they will fit snugly into any building noble enough to have pillars.

CHAPTER XXV

TRAVEL

ABROAD. To choose a travelling companion solely for his or her artistic appreciation is the height of folly. Even though both of you have the same tastes in pictures and are equally able to discuss the pros and cons of baroque architecture, if one of you wants the window up and the other one wants it down your trip is doomed to failure.

If you have a preference for five-star hotels and good plumbing do not choose a friend who thinks it is much more fun to go to that little place you saw near the station, l'Ane Rouge, so that you can buy lots of *éclairs* with the money saved.

If you are punctual and the type of person who rises early to pack, making small scratching noises with

N

paper as of a mouse furnishing her nest, do not select
as a companion one who gets up half an hour before
the train leaves and hurls things loose into bags, packing the overflow into hastily constructed parcels and
giving you the residue to carry.

If you dislike emotional scenes do not travel with a
fearless arguer, a creature who refuses to be over-
charged or overpersuaded or diddled in any way. The
English voice angrily raised in a foreign tongue can
only be borne by those equally angry; indeed it is not
etiquette to be vexed abroad, not out loud, that is.
After bewailing, in private, the foreign system of increasing the prices, dismantling the baths, erupting
the roads and filling the canals with putrescent matter
at the mere approach of a Briton, it is etiquette to pay
up, to go unwashed, to make a detour and to hold the
nose in absolute silence. The British were born to be
discomfited.

If you are the sort of person who looks to guides for
historical information do not journey with a confirmed
Baedeker reader as there is bound to be an ugly clash
of wills. A Baedeker lover *must* have a stooge to whom
he can read, and if he is thwarted in any way a feeling
of resentment curdles inside him eventually to emerge
in the form of derogatory remarks of a personal nature.
It is essential to his happiness to have someone to tell
him if the stained glass window he is reading about is

really there; whether the left panel does in fact depict the overthrow of the Antichrist and the right panel St Jerome handing a fish to the Bishop of Savona, for it is quite impossible for a fervent Baedeker reader to raise his head and look for himself. The moment he does so he loses his place in the book. Which is ghastly. It is essential he should have a sort of yesman who will lie on his back in the nave and tell him if really and truly the apostles, the angels with instruments, the patriarchs, the virgins and the martyrs which should by rights be on the ceiling are indeed there, and that he is reading the correct page about the correct edifice. Thus re-assured he can be led, his eyes and forefinger still glued to the book, out into the sunshine (or, of course, the rain) a happy man. Plant him anywhere on earth indeed, and provided his scarlet bible is in his hand he will be happy. "Look!" you cry, "what a lovely lake!" "H'm . . ." he replies, flipping the pages in a frenzy of eagerness, ". . . ah yes, here we are. It says that until recently the only outlet for the waters was a drain constructed in the fifteenth century, but this gradually became choked up. A second drain on the site of an old tunnel was accordingly made in 1896, to regulate the height of the water and to diminish the sway of fever. A project for draining it entirely, formed by Napoleon, was given up". "Really?" you say. "Yes, really!" he says, flushed with joy.

Another vital issue in the choosing of travelling companions is that of endurance. It is all very well to cry with Milton, "Oh let my due feet never fail to walk the studious cloisters pale", yet it is common knowledge that even the best cloisters, if studied for too long, wring from the lips of sightseers a different cry, one that was wrung from Lord Tennyson after he had been taken to see the daisies at the bottom of Maud's garden for the third time in one afternoon: "I am aweary, aweary, oh God, that I were dead!" Friends with fallen arches are best left at home, unless of course you yourself happen to have fallen arches, in which case it is an excellent idea to choose a friend who has something called either "my back" or "after my operation". The perfect sightseer is one who starts thinking about a cup of hot chocolate at precisely the same minute as you do, and whose interest in Tiepolo flags the identical second your shoes begin to pinch. Incidentally, it is a curious thing that nearly all great works of art are commemorated by the food one eats before or after seeing them; indeed it is sometimes the only way one can remember them at all. If, after you have returned home, someone says to you, "Do you remember that wonderful staircase we saw at Amboise?" you may burst your brains in vain, but if, noting the mental struggles you are undergoing, he adds, "You *know*, where we had the strawberry flan?"

memory will instantly return. Depressing though it may be for those who deem the spirit to be stronger than the flesh, the fact must be bravely faced that a cathedral juxtaposed with a delicious *bouillabaisse* or a château contiguous with a bad smell of drains is infinitely easier to recall than those one viewed between meals, unscented.

There may be occasions when the traveller is invited to eat with a native. England is the only civilised country in the world where it is etiquette to fall on the food like a wolf the moment it is served. Elsewhere it is *comme il faut* to wait until everybody has helped himself to everything and until everything on everybody's plate is stone cold. Then you can wade in. It is a much fairer system because in this way you all start even and it is the quickest eater and not the first served who gets first crack at a second helping. English people who try to take advantage of this, pleading ignorance or obstinacy, and start sucking up the soup while it is still hot, are rotten sports. They should be horsewhipped.

It is permissible abroad to wipe one's plate with a piece of bread.

In some eastern instances, it is obligatory to eat with one's fingers.

With chopsticks it is impossible to eat anything at all.

Sitting cross-legged on the ground with a sheik it is

advisable to eat everything offered, sheep's eyes, camel's tongues and old pieces of grey flannel included. One never knows when a sheik may take offence.

Do not be surprised, when you are dining with European acquaintances, to find a little glass *je ne sais quoi* nestling against the cutlery. This is a knife rest or *couteau repos* and after you have eaten the *viande* you wipe your knife on a *morceau de pain* and lay it there ready for use on the *camembert* or the *pâté de foie gras* or anything else you may have the good fortune to be offered. Although it is considered wasteful to use more than one knife at a meal, forks are allowed a certain latitude, and so are spoons. You can use as many of them as you want, but when you have finished with them it is etiquette to abandon them in a haphazard fashion on your plate. The regimentation of cutlery is *verboten*. Just drop the things anywhere.

There is one small snag in taking meals with the French. It is *un petit rien* but unless it is noted it is apt to instil an odour of mystery into an otherwise ordinary repast. When you have drunk your post-prandial cup of coffee, your hostess will probably say to you "*Vous voulez encore, chère madame?*" Translating, with the rapidity of sheeted lightning, the English word "Thanks" into the French word "*Merci*", you say it. "*Merci*", you say. Now whatever views you may have on the word "*merci*", however many times you may have bandied it about without hurting anybody (indeed it has been one of your most successful *bon mots*), on this occasion, for some inexplicable, occult, Gallic reason it means N O. You will *not* get your coffee. In order to do so you just think of some other sparkling words, such as, "Oh, wee, wee, seel vous play", or "J'aimeray beaucoup avoir ongcor".

If you are observant and conspicuously on the *qui vive* you will notice that foreign guests at a luncheon or dinner party often tip the maid as they gather up their hats and coats to go. This may throw you into a flutter, but do not let it. If you start indulging in this sort of whimsicality your trips abroad will be seriously curtailed, and in the face of the present currency regulations it is better to brush the whole thing aside. Be blind. Be stupid. Be British. Be careful.

In the days of our youth it was considered an invitation to death to drink foreign water unless it was in a bottle. It was noted that foreigners were not overfond of the element themselves and preferred wine, which made it all frightfully suspicious; but now that every coin has to be counted, re-counted and weighed against the balance of a suspender belt, the custom of carrying bottles of Evian and Fuggi about with one has lapsed. A lot of tepid tap water has trickled down a lot of delicate British throats these past years, and no one has been any the worse for it. Perhaps it is not absolutely etiquette to drink water lifted straight from the Nile in a sardine tin as do the Egyptians, but there is no need to continue the practice of throwing the salad out of the window because it must have been washed in a "sink of iniquity".

In the United States it is correct always to carry the mouth a little open. Wonder should be your constant companion, praise be given lavishly and good humour be rampant at all times. It is etiquette for the British to live at the expense of Americans and hope to pay them back some day. This is highly illegal, but etiquette. A nice balance must be struck between eating too much and eating too little, between exclaiming rapturously at the fried chicken and not noticing it. To appear starving is to suggest that one is cadging for food parcels, while to seem surfeited is to forfeit the chance of getting sent any.

The sight of other English people abroad is apt to be depressing, particularly as they always behave in such an irresponsible manner and wear such frightful clothes. To see disembarking on some distant shore a boat load of British subjects, lobster pink and bursting through their cricket blazers with *bonhomie*, is a truly terrible experience and it is an added anguish to hear them speak. Travel seems not only to broaden the mind but also to loosen the vocal chords, and it is apparently necessary to greet people with whom one has been in close contact every day for a week with such joyful and excited screams that the notes of them reverberate down the streets of foreign cities in a way unheard of at home. There is a lamentable feeling of *laissez aller* amongst these wayfarers and however loud your own voice may be or, for that matter, your own blazer, it is etiquette to eye all organised tours of your fellow-countrymen with the strongest distaste.

There is, however, the matter of that couple in your hotel. You know who they are because they are always being photographed by *The Tatler* marking their race cards at Newmarket, and you can see by the guarded way they look at your feet that they *think* they know you, or at any rate you're the sort of type of person who might be a friend of friends of their. The etiquette on this occasion is to cut each other dead for two days, nod on the third, borrow a match on the fourth, converse on meteorological probabilities on the fifth, discover you have dozens of mutual friends on the evening of the sixth and leave on the morning of the seventh.

AT HOME. Since tissue paper went out of commission, packing has become comparatively simple. In the old days it was etiquette to wrap up each item separately and if possible so to disguise its contours that if, in the course of a journey, it became necessary to dip into a suitcase for a pocket handkerchief, one was quite incapable of distinguishing it from the bottle of brilliantine or the toothpaste. Many a railway compartment and the passengers seated therein became submerged in sheaves of snowy paper as some wretched creature, in quest of a simple piece of cambric, tore at the packages with palsied fingers, hurled from her the wrappings which encased her nightgown, wrenched apart the coverings which concealed her stockings, only to end by wiping her nose on her evening slip. But these days are past. Nevertheless, it is still *à la mode* to put sponges in a sponge bag and shoes at the bottom of the case, unless of course you have overlooked them till the last moment, when it is *à la mode* to put them loose on top. There is much to be said for being able to recognise the objects you have packed when you come to unpack them, but against this happy nakedness must be weighed the disadvantage of having no expendable material into which the objects can leak. It is very second-rate to wear a suit soaked in whisky or a dress incarnadined with nail varnish. A shirt impregnated with hair lotion is taboo in even the lowest circles. It is safest to make a little cache of combustibles in one corner of the receptacle and to build a wall of solids round it, though to tell the truth Chanel No. 5 on the tennis shoes is not absolutely etiquette either.

Travellers who like fresh air have precedence over those who don't. This is based on the vague idea that

English air must be a good thing, and on the less vague idea that they will probably be sick if the window is shut. Only the most blatantly effete dare to suggest closing a window, except of course in a tunnel. As tunnels cannot be anticipated, the carriage is invariably filled with black sulphurous smoke, which would not matter at all save for the fact that it is unfortunately necessary to open the window again to let it out.

It is a mistake to assume that you and your friends are the only people in a public vehicle who can understand a foreign tongue. Even bus conductors have, during this past decade, learned through circumstances beyond their control, a few words of French or German, therefore it is unwise, even one might say unhealthy, to pass such a remark as "Tiens, on dirait un crapeau, n'est-ce pas . . . celui-là avec les yeux croisés?" Nearly three-quarters of England's population are semi-illiterate, but they are not yet dumb, and having picked up some exceptionally rude words from their brothers overseas they will not hesitate to use them. Your mink coat will no longer protect you, in fact it will be a goad, so unless you know some pretty rude words yourself, which of course is extremely unlikely, do not pass personal remarks in anything but Erse, Chinese or Volapuk.

CHAPTER XXVI

QUEUING

ALTHOUGH a queue is etiquette, the etiquette for queuing is still in a somewhat fluid stage and it will take another decade before it has crystallised into a recognisable shape. As a matter of fact at the moment the queue itself is often shapeless and the minds of those queuing equally as amorphous, so much so that many a housewife, her wits battered by life's bludgeons into a sort of dreamy putty, may join a queue the purpose of which she is unaware, and shuffle forwards to the purchase of something she does not want, simply because it is "done".

Those who jump queues may get the last Swiss roll but they will be the first to wish they hadn't. It is a sad insight into the human heart as it thumps to-day to note that even those bearing priority cards testifying to illness, old age or imminent maternity are relegated to hell by those more physically fortunate out of whom they have cheated the last slice of rock salmon.

Neither invective nor fists need be employed to rebuke the froward. The modest phrase "I think I was here before *you*!" can sound like a battle-cry in the mouth of a roused counter-reacher, or even the words "Excuse *me*!" can, if properly articulated, charge the air with such venom that the culprit reels away and totters past a battery of condemning eyes to the end of the queue.

The etiquette for queuing for buses is very obscure, for though it is based theoretically on the rule of first come first bussed, in practice those behind invariably get home long before those in front. This is because they want the No. 15 which arrives in triplicate, and the front of the queue wants the No. 8A which hardly ever arrives at all. It is arranged that the No. 15s, which serve the backs of queues, should stop well short of the bus stop and that the No. 8As, which serve the fronts of queues, should stop several yards beyond it. This enables prospective passengers to run along the gutters in contrary directions, shouting and hitting each other with umbrellas. The reintegration of those who have failed to gain their objective (*a*) because the conductor vowed there were no empty seats on top, (*b*) because he started the bus before any-one had time to reach it, (*c*) because they quite simply got knocked down, is a difficult problem, the solution of which depends largely upon the size and fitness of the protagonists.

While we are on the subject of buses let there be noted some points of etiquette for those who are eventually bus-borne. This being the age of reason it is often reasoned by gentlemen that as ladies strive so hard to be equal with men in all things, especially pay, they must take the rough with the smooth and learn to stand on their own feet, or at any rate only on the toes of others. What gentlemen forget, however, is that this much-to-be-desired equality has not yet been achieved. It is still a dream, a vision, a miasma, and as gentlemen are not keen on the idea anyway they can be subtly unhelpful by continuing, as in the old days, to treat their women like delicate china. This will take the ladies' minds off their emancipation and the weight off their legs. Gentlemen should realise that when they offer their seats to ladies, and not *only* to pretty ones, a wave of kindliness surges through the bus like a breath of spring air. They become the per-sonification of Chivalry. It is true that everyone stares at them because it is such an extraordinary thing to do, but if they get too embarrassed they can always pre-tend they are getting out at the next stop. As for ladies themselves, their manners should be regulated by age and avoirdupois, the young and thin rising for the old and fat. *Everybody* should rise for a baby in arms, and, if possible, evacuate the bus, for heaven's sake.

There are no queues, no manners and no etiquette for Tube travelling. It is a free for all and let the sliding doors take the hindmost.